MILLIONAIRE MINDSET:

TIPS ON MAKING AND KEEPING MONEY

Ibikunle Fayemi

Published by:

Ibikunle Fayemi

5, Tijani Bello Street, Ojodu-Ikeja, Lagos, South-West Nigeria.
+2348127718107 and +2348033511207

FOREWORD

Wealth can do more for mankind than poverty. With wealth i.e. financial wealth, the possessor can spend from it to fulfill his or her needs or wants while creating income for the supplier of those needs or wants. The wealthy can also directly expend their wealth for the betterment of others. Wealth made through ethical means is a capital for the good of human beings, and everyone should strive to get it. How can this wealth be garnered, created, made to become more and be sustained?

This book, "Millionaire Mindset: Tips on Making and Keeping Money", provides the foundational structure for wealth generation. It posits rightly that becoming a millionaire begins with a mindset, a paradigm. It addresses the solving of various defects of the mind for anyone who wants to develop a millionaire mindset. All through its chapters, this book reinforces the need to keep the mind off thoughts that are inimical to wealth accumulation and preservation. This dimension is not often considered in most African societies, including Nigeria, where everything is left for God.

Chapter 1 Bidding Poverty Goodbye invites the reader to hate poverty and all its consequences. Chapter 2 Developing The Millionaire Mindset invites the readers to what he or she needs to know in developing a millionaire mindset. While it is good to hate poverty and all its consequences, and the importance to know, Chapter 3 Decision Decides Destination is a challenge to focus on making wealth. Decision-making is critical. Chapter 4 Time is Money emphasizes the importance of the universal resource "Time" in the making of wealth. It draws the reader to re-evaluate how he or she uses his or her time.

Chapter 5 Savings re-echoes the time-tested culture of anyone who ever resolved to set out to become wealthy. Savings are the seeds. Chapter 6 deals with planting these seeds – Investing. This chapter on investing shows some investment outlets and cautions on scams being made to look like investing opportunities that must be avoided. Certain values or associations may affect an intending investor or an actual investor. This is the import of chapter 7 Associate with Like Mind/Law of Attraction. Chapter 8 Creating Wealth shares the amazing story of Jeff Bezos whose meteoric rise has displaced, at one time or the other, the inspiring position of Bill Gates as the world's wealthiest. The chapter shows practically the demands of creating wealth and shares the various powers, some of which can be tapped in creating wealth. It also highlights the need to master and implement the input-process-output for wealth creation.

For those operating or seeking to serve in politics or public governance, chapter 9 Millionaire Mindset in Politics exposes the sine qua non principles for this attainment. Chapter 10 Nature Versus Nurture re-inforces the need for us the readers to take the responsibility to work our way out to success irrespective of what nature has given us. It is a call to a can-do spirit for freedom. Chapter 11 Health is Wealth alerts us to keep healthy in pursuit of our financial wealth goal. It reaffirms that health should not be traded off, or tampered with in quest for financial wealth. Chapter 12 Contentment As A Reward caps the book up as the hallmark of truly millionaire minds. It posits that the successfully wealthy or those with the ideal millionaire mindset are fulfilled at every stage they are, even as they push for more.

I once enrolled for a master's degree programme which included a course on wealth creation. The lecturer assigned to teach/lecture on financial management and wealth, without any pun intended, looked and lived nothing like what he was tutoring on. He was very poor, and only repeated what he read about finance and wealth but lacked the millionaire mindset. In hindsight, the programme was an unethical opportunistic platform to milk innocent students – it expressed a scarcity and lack mindset. Of course, I happily dropped out. While reading this book, although acknowledging certain individual differences, I smiled at the reality of the facts shared, not the ideals I paid significantly for, to hear from lecturers whose economic lives do not authenticate what they tried to sell to me. I cherish real-life book like this.

Mr. Ibikunle Fayemi is commended for sharing his insights, drawing from his observations and personal financial life experiences in Nigeria and in United States, for those swimming in the ocean of poverty to swim their way out. This book is recommended for this set of people and for all haters of poverty, and everything associated with it. It is a book written by a blunt Nigerian who crafted his path to financial freedom. I wish all the readers of this book a happy reading that will trigger implementation towards crafting their paths to wealth.

O.J. Samuel
Founder & CEO, O.J. Samuel Books Ltd
Ikeja
Lagos
Nigeria

O.J. Samuel, Samuel Joseph Okoye, is a chartered accountant, tax consultant and ex-banker who uses his background to drive entrepreneurship education and passive income creation in Nigeria. He is author of several books and he is on a mission to inspire and challenge people to do the 'impossible' and become more. He can be reached through accsam2005@yahoo.com and 09030770109.

APPRECIATION

I will like to thank Prince Adeyemi Wilson Moyele Adewole. Mr. Wilson, as he is fondly called, taught me the art of goodness. He is one of those Christians that not only talk the talk, but also walk the walk. He is a special breed, a good judge of people, yet nonjudgmental. His millionaire mindset is worthy of emulation.

Also, I will like to thank Mrs. Mubo Fawale Adegoke. Mrs. Adegoke is the Chief Executive Officer of MMB Caterers. A genuinely generous patriot with a rare human kindness, she is an epitome of a modern woman with a millionaire mindset.

I have known Temidayo Solanke for many years. He is the CEO of Hannah-ice Nigeria Limited, Jazz 38 Bus Stop, Plot CC Block 115, T.F Kuboye Road, Lekki Phase 1, Ocean Side, Lagos. Dayo is hardworking, loyal, and honest. Diligence, the constant and earnest effort to accomplish whatever is undertaken, is Dayo's middle name. His commitment to diligence has helped him to achieve great things in life. This commitment to diligence has rewarded him with expertise and authority in his chosen field. He has hugely demonstrated that there is no short cut to success. I watched him over the years developing the millionaire mindset. I am not only watching him now enjoying the proceeds of his hard work, I am also taking a delicious bite out of his manifested sweet success. Thank you Dayo.

Finally, I will like to thank one of the pillars of DOOR. DOOR is the acronym for Defining Our Own Reality. Tokunbo Tonade is a rare, sparkling gem in the midst of his contemporaries. A silent patriot with an encased spirit of truth, Tokunbo's new dream to build an estate powered by solar using his second company named Fossidgrag Nig Limited is a blessing to a country that is still bedeviled with electric power outage. I appreciate his propensity for balanced and critical thinking and his knack for quietly empowering others.

DEDICATION

I have many friends with the millionaire mindset. But Olakunle Salako stands tall among them. He is one of the most hardworking, most enterprising people that I know.

This book is dedicated to my long time friend, Olakunle Salako. He taught me what friendship looked like, not with mere words, but with actions reeking with love and genuine affection.

I remember when we were both student pilots at Boardmans Flight Academy in Fort-Worth, Texas, United States. We both decided to travel back to Nigeria in December of 1981. I was younger, smaller, but with a bigger luggage. He was older, bigger, but with a smaller baggage. When he saw me struggling with my bigger luggage, he volunteered to carry my luggage and he gave me his smaller one.

Many years later, I went to spend the night in his house in Lagos, Nigeria. There was no electric light that night but he turned on his generator and I slept nicely, with the air conditioner on, without mosquitoes. The next morning, I went to his room. And it was hot. Why? His generator could only carry one air conditioner. He chose not to sleep with air conditioner so that I could sleep with one. That action re-set my brain on how to treat a good friend.

A good friend is a social capital that is as good as financial capital. In all your getting, get a good friend. I have one. And his name is Olakunle Salako. He deserves some accolades.

TABLE OF CONTENT

INTRODUCTION

The love of money is said to be the root of all evil. This may be true to certain extent. We have seen all types of evil deeds being carried out by human beings in their desperate attempts to make money at all cost.

The story of billionaire kidnapper, Chukwudubem Onwuamadike – aka Evans, is an example of the love of money being the root of all evil. He was arrested in June, 2017 by the police for coordinating several high-profile kidnappings, armed robbery and murder within Lagos, Edo, Abia, Enugu and Anambra States. Evans, a native of Akamili, Umudim Quarters, Nnewi, Anambra State, dropped out of school while in Junior Secondary School Class 2, when his father, Steven Onwuamadike, drove his mother, Chinwe, away and got married to another woman. He came to Lagos where he joined a robbery gang that specialized in attacking luxury buses plying the East-West Road, at night. Evans and his gang usually attacked these buses on the highway and dispossessed the passengers of their cash and other valuables. Some of his gang members were later arrested and when the police were closing in on him, he fled the country only to return a few years later and relocated to the East. After raising enough money, he travelled to South Africa. On his return, he veered into full time kidnapping with Lagos as his base. He used to pose as a spare parts dealer from South Africa with proceeds from his crime. Some people lost their lives in the hands of Evans, who is currently standing trial for kidnapping at the time this book is being published.

However, money is also said to answer all things. No matter how compassionate we are, without some type of money, it may be very difficult for us to help those we feel compassionate about. Some people may think it does not matter where they get money from. I think it matters. Making money by harming others or their interests creates a kind of imbalance in a society. If it is true that "It really does not matter how you get it" (money), won't criticizing ritualist, armed robbers and kidnappers for corruptly enriching themselves be hypocritical?

Money gives us purchasing power. It gives us the power to purchase what we desire. The acquisition of the things we desire makes us happy. Yes, money has the power to make us happy. How happy can we be without money, with bills pilling up, with children to feed? Not very happy but downright depressing, I will say. How many of us can truthfully say that a bank credit alert does not alter his/her mood? Money is not happiness, agreed but money is a vital element of happiness. The ability to manage money well is very vital to success and happiness. To be able to get what we need, the things we want, we need money.

Two people can have exactly the same amount of money and feel totally different. One may feel it is enough. The other may feel it is not. Their financial burdens may be the determinant factor here. The less financial burden one carries, the less money he/she will need and, the happier one will be. As human beings, we have many needs that have to be satisfied if we are to be comfortable and content. The satisfaction of these needs requires money. According to Abraham Maslow, humans have five needs that we must continually satisfy if we are to continuously enjoy the simple pleasures of life. The following is Maslow Hierarchy of Needs.

Physiological needs are said to include air, food, water, shelter, warmth, sleep, etc. Safety needs include shelter, security, law & order, employment, health, stability, etc. Love/Belonging needs include belongingness, love, affection, intimacy, family, friends, relationships, etc. Examples of esteem needs are self-esteem, self-confidence, achievement, recognition, status, respect, etc. And, at the top of the hierarchy of these human needs is self-actualizing needs. These are realizing one's personal potential, self-fulfillment; pursue talent, personal growth, peak experiences, creativity, etc. Naturally, human beings are motivated to satisfy lower needs before higher needs can be addressed. How can these needs be satisfied without money? The simple answer to that question is: it is impossible for the modern humans to satisfy their needs without money.

The best way not to achieve financial freedom is to focus on the wrong things. We can blame, wail, and curse all day, pointing accusing finger at those that are supposedly causing our woes and worries. But if we do not correct the real causes of those woes and worries, no problem may get solved. Our powerlessness may be the chief culprit in most of our woes and worries. And if you are satisfied with the results you have been getting so far, there is no need for argument. Continue to do as you know if you already love the results you are getting. We can indeed tell a tree from the fruits it bears. Making decisions in life without stress and worry about financial impact is to be financially free. Controlling your finance instead of letting it control you is to be financially free. Cutting your coat according to your fabrics is to be financially free. "The happiest life is the one which contains the least financial burden."

A lot of people are already shouldering more than normal financial burden. And we all know that money is in short supply all over the country. Yet, some people are still making decisions of their own, or accepting the decisions of others, that increase their financial burden even further. The result of this is, poverty, begging, and borrowing. Solution? Shrink your appetites. Expand your scruples. Self-discipline. Self-control. Self-denial. Use them and see how simple life becomes. A lot of decisions have financial implications. Do not allow those that will not carry the financial burden attached to decisions to decide for you. I always strive so that my decisions never leave a leak in other people's pocket. Also, I always make sure that other people's decisions never leave a leak in my pocket. He who dictates the tune must pay the pipers.

Are your decisions leading you towards financial freedom or away from it? Do you have money saved up for rainy days? Do you invest a portion of your income? Do you have effective money management skills? Financial management refers to the efficient and effective management of money in such a manner as to accomplish one's objectives and goals. Do you want to start and manage your own business? Are you working towards financial freedom? If your answers to all these questions are in the affirmative, then this book is for you.

You can become a multi-millionaire by meeting or creating great demand for a real service or product. A mere belief that you can become a multi-millionaire alone does not mean you can. In order to develop a millionaire mindset, a precondition to becoming a multi-millionaire, you have to become goal-orientated. You have to live within or below your means in the beginning. You must convert your extra money into investments in your self-development or in other business ventures. Continuous learning is also a must for you.

The beauty of the financial knowledge you will get from this book is that it will make you to do better, financially, than you were doing before you acquire this knowledge. To improve your finance, you have to improve the quality of your knowledge, and consequently, the quality of your decisions. This will ultimately improve the quality of your life. Financial decisions are often life decisions. Therefore, link your financial goals to your life's goals. Making good financial decisions and acting on them is wisdom. Getting favorable and desirable financial results is the reward of this wisdom. Inasmuch as the environment can influence our financial decision-making, our decisions too can tremendously influence the environment.

A lot of financial advice is straightforward and simple ("earn more, spend less.") Simple as it is, it is not easy. Work with the practical knowledge you will get from this book to develop the quality of your financial decision-making. Self-discipline, self-control, focus, are some of the vital tools you will need. Without self-discipline and focus, nothing worthwhile can be achieved in life. Even when a seemingly achievement is attained, it will be unsustainable.

If you want financial growth and progress, you have to change some of your behaviors that are not conducive to financial growth and progress. Financial success is just about behavior as much as it is about skills. If you keep on doing what you have always done, you may keep on getting what you have always gotten. Spending is sweet. We all know that. Having money to spend is fun. Even children will attest to this. But bad spending habits that leave one broke is sour. This book will teach you how to adopt sound strategies for saving that will exempt you from being broke in the coming tough days. There are tough days ahead, no doubt. But with prudent financial planning, we can scale through the tough times unscathed. Start saving for those tough times ahead. Remember that a naira saved today is also a naira earned in the future.

Ultimately, this book will explain how we can satisfy our human needs by making and keeping the type of money that answers all things while steering clear of its evil roots.

CHAPTER 1

BIDDING POVERTY GOODBYE

"We choose our joys and sorrows long before we experience them..." ~ **Khalil Gibran.**

The benefits of money in our lives are very obvious. Money is what puts roofs over our heads. It is what puts food on the tables. Similarly, it is what we use to provide assistance for our family and friends. Therefore, anyone that consistently lacks money needs to look inward and resolve the problem that is creating the lack. Stop for a minute. Look around you. See those poor, old miserable people? Yes, they were once young, like you, and full of life, full of hopes. They once believed, in "God", and in themselves. Yet they still ended up, in their old age, poor, miserable, and sometimes loveless. What went wrong? At some point in their lives, they made life-ruining mistakes. And they eventually stopped learning. They stopped growing. And some of us may, unconsciously, be making the same life-ruining mistakes. We may have stopped learning. We may have stopped growing. We need to become conscious of these mistakes, and we need to correct them before it is too late. Poor decision making is one of the factors that create poverty. A well-knitted lifestyle must be planned and not just hoped for. Proper planning is known to prevent poor performance. It is not anyone's destiny to be poor. Ignorance, lack of focus, and lack of self discipline are mostly responsible.

What is poverty? Poverty is not having enough money to meet

basic needs like food, clothing and shelter. A lot of people face poverty and find it difficult to overcome. The World Bank Organization describes poverty thus: "Poverty is hunger. Poverty is lack of shelter. Poverty is being sick and not being able to see a doctor. Poverty is not having access to school and not knowing how to read. Poverty is not having a job, is fear for the future, living one day at a time. Poverty has many faces, changing from place to place and across time, and has been described in many ways. Most often, poverty is a situation people want to escape. So poverty is a call to action -- for the poor and the wealthy alike -- a call to change the world so that many more may have enough to eat, adequate shelter, access to education and health, protection from violence, and a voice in what happens in their communities."

A poor person is not able to afford many things. He is unable to participate in recreational activities with his friends. He is not able to send his children on excursion with their schoolmates. Buying new clothes for the same children is difficult for him. When he is sick, he is not able to buy medications for the sickness. I opine that anyone that is intelligent, with good education and pertinent knowledge can overcome poverty by hard work and stay away from poverty forever.

Some poor people believe they are suffering from "ogun idile", a Yoruba phrase for generational curse. This is not true. They are actually suffering from generational ignorance, and, what they need is total psychological formatting. The formatting is to rid them of the erroneous thinking/beliefs that is preventing them from acquiring the required mindset, knowledge and skills to create wealth. When they take the time to learn how to change that thinking/beliefs and become a better thinker, they are investing in themselves. "If you want to amend your errors, you must begin by amending your philosophy." ~ **Jim Rohn.**

I inherited poverty just like anyone else who did. In my attempt to get rid of poverty, I beckoned on illegality for assistance. That was after I lost patience with the right and legal path. For a while, illegality earned me a fortune. It gave me the illusion that I had banished poverty. I became profligate. I forgot the fundamental rules of finance. I departed from the basic principles that guaranteed the continuous enjoyment of life. And, guess what? Reality eventually reared its head. The truth caught up with the lie. I was flung back in time, about twenty years, to go and begin again. The patience I did not have naturally was imposed on me by the universal law of cause and effect. Imagine that. Bidding poverty goodbye forever is a process. This process requires pertinent knowledge and skills. Acquire these knowledge and skills and begin to lay the foundation for, not only your own wealth, but also that of your future generation.

Mental models are deeply ingrained assumptions and generalizations that influence how we understand the world. Until these are brought to the surface and thoroughly scrutinized, little knowledge takes place that does not conform to these models. If your mental models are not solving a lot of your problems, you need a paradigm shift. What is a Paradigm Shift? A paradigm shift is when a significant change happens, usually from one fundamental view to a different view. In most cases, some type of major discontinuity occurs as well. Our beliefs are essentially our mental models. Beliefs initiate and guide actions. Beliefs can either guide actions in the right direction or in the wrong direction. "Suppose you want to arrive at a specific location in central Chicago, a street map of the city would be a great help to you in reaching your destination. But, suppose you were given the wrong map. Through a printing error, the map labeled 'Chicago' was actually a map for Detroit. Can you imagine the frustration, the ineffectiveness of trying to reach your destination? You might work on your behavior---you could try harder, be more diligent, double your speed. But your efforts would only succeed in getting you to the wrong place faster. You might work in your attitude---you could think more positively. You still won't get to the right place, but perhaps you won't care. Your attitude would be so positive, but you'd still be lost. The fundamental problem has nothing to do with your behavior or your attitude. It has everything to do with having the wrong map. If you have the right map of Chicago, then diligence becomes important, and when you encounter frustrating obstacles on the way, then attitude can make a real difference. But the first and most important requirement is the accuracy of the map." ~ **7 Habits of Highly Effective People.**

The mental maps---mental models--- in your head have to be in alignment with the true knowledge of creating wealth. This is how to bid poverty goodbye forever. To bid poverty goodbye forever, you need to be fully tuned in to learning new knowledge and skills, or improve upon the existing ones. Minimize distractions as much as possible. If you are twenty years behind someone, and you keep on doing the same thing the person is doing, the same way, you will always be behind that person. To catch up, or even pass that person, you need to do something positively different.

Imagine a man that works as a gateman of a private house. His basic pay per month is eighteen thousand naira (18k.) To supplement his salary, he washes about ten cars a day. He also shines shoes. He is obviously a hardworking guy, not the lazy type. But he has two wives, six kids. And he may still make more kids. After all, "God" is the provider of children. He has nine mouths to feed from the sweat of his labour. And that may increase in the nearest future. He may have locked himself, and his family, inside the palace of poverty. And he may have thrown the key away. Sometimes, poverty is a self-inflicted disease that only prudent practice, self-discipline, self-control can cure. It is possible for someone with a better paying job than the gateman to fall in the same palace of poverty as the gateman if expenses exceed income. Frolicking inside the palace of poverty, with no escape route, leads to perpetual poverty. It ought not to be so for prudent people. Caveat: always cut your coat according to your fabrics or poverty will always eat deep into your soul. If it is only one child you can conveniently cater for, by all means, have only one child. Bringing children into the world to suffer economic hardship is not a responsible act.

It may be delusional to make decisions without having corresponding power/resources to carry out the decisions. When our desires exceed our power/resources, our mind is susceptible to all sorts of negativity, delusion included. We leave ourselves open to manipulation by others offering perpetual promise of everlasting solution. Promises that are perpetual: just promises. As an initial matter, shrink your desires to the limit of your power/resources. Then, find creative ways to grow within the scope of your limitations. It is not nice for our children to inherit poverty in a country where most things do not work well. Begin to lay the foundation for your family generational wealth.

Good money management is very essential to getting out of poverty and creating wealth. The first step in getting rich is to start saving money. A naira saved is a naira earned. Live below your income until you have become rich. Stop faking it before you make it. A lot of people are broke because they are spending more money than they are making. Be proactive. Stop the blame game. "It's your parents fault for making you who you are, and it's your fault for staying that way." Do what is absolutely necessary to bid poverty goodbye forever. I have never met anyone who set out to fail or to be poor. Yet people fail everyday in large numbers. And there are poor people all over the country. Why? Because they may have learned, unwittingly, thinking and habits that invariably lead to failure, to poverty. Solution? (1) Identifying the thinking and habits that invariably lead to failure, to poverty. (2) Unlearning those thinking and behavior. (3) Relearning thinking and behavior that ultimately lead to success, to creating wealth. (4) Striving to do the right things the right way in all things at all times. Lack, begging, suffering at old age are consequences for a youth that does not know how to manage money well.

You must have a clear practical plan to bid poverty goodbye forever. What do you need? What can you do to get what you need? Do you have the required knowledge and skills to do it? Can you do that thing exceeding well? Does it pay well? What do you love to do? If you want to be successful, you have to love what you do. That thing you love to do is your passion. Passion is defined as "strong and barely controllable emotion." Are you good at what you love to do? Do you have the adequate knowledge and skills? Is it ethical? That thing that you love to do, that you are good at doing, and that is ethical, does it pay well? If your answers to the last four questions are yes, you are ready to climb the ladder of success and happiness.

What does the world need? Does that thing the world need pay very well? Are you good at that thing the world needs? Do you have the required knowledge and skills to produce it? I have met a young man who had a B.Sc in Physics and did not know what the 'scientific method" meant. He graduated from a Nigerian university. He said he was not taught what the scientific method was. Tell me how he could grow and progress as a physicist when he did not have the required basic knowledge of his profession. Bidding poverty goodbye is not just about being half-educated. It is about being well educated. It is about being able to perform the core function of one's profession exceedingly well. Use the present power you have to correct the errors you see in your life. You are not as powerless as you think. We all have "hidden human resources" that can be developed. These are called talents. But stick to ideas you can do something about. The following is a fictional story of what can happen if you plan without having the required knowledge to execute the plan:

Who will Bell the Cat?

A story was told of how a cat was disturbing a bunch of rats. The rats got together to find solution to their problem. A supposedly smart rat came up with a supposedly smart plan: the rats should tie a bell around the neck of the cat. The jingles of the bell would then alert the rats whenever the cat was around. Every rat jumped for joy. What a brilliant idea. Then reality hit. "Who will bell the cat?" Moral of the story is: Ideals are good but practicality is what always matters.

Recognizing a problem is good. But grasping the cause and consequences is better. The best is moving swiftly to solve the problem and putting mechanisms in place to prevent future occurrence. So, have you recognized your problems? Everyone has one to a certain degree. Can you realistically identify the cause and consequences, without recourse to pointing finger outward but inward? Are you able to afford many things? Are you able to participate in recreational activities with your friends? Are you able to send your children on excursion with their schoolmates? Buying new clothes for the same children is easy for you? When you are sick, are you able to buy medications for the sickness? What are the things you are doing to solve these problems if you have them? And what are the mechanisms you will put in place to prevent future occurrence? Remember that, anything left by itself will go from bad to worse. I opine that anyone that is intelligent, with good education and pertinent knowledge can overcome poverty by hard work. He can banish poverty forever. The time of adversity can truly lead to the determination to do away with the wrong decisions, false beliefs, and negative mentality that led one into the adversity. "Deal with your problems before they deal with your happiness." This is the right time to bid poverty goodbye forever. This is the right time to develop The Millionaire Mindset. Stop waiting. And start doing, yes, with whatever you have. Focus on yourself. Become a better you. Be more competent, less corrupt. Think creatively, innovatively. Change certain things in your life. Be more financially prudent, less wasteful.

I hope you have now realized that the first step in banishing poverty for good is to get a sound education. The ability to learn from your past mistakes is probably one of the best ways to learn. Invest in continuous learning and invest in the education of your children. Next step is to associate with like minds that will help in making right decisions in business or investments. Start saving money immediately if you have not been doing so already. You are going to need capital to move to the next level. I think lack of money is one of the root causes of all evil. Resolve not to be poor. Whatever your income is at present, try to spend less so that your can have extra to save. The accumulation of that savings is what you will use as investment to make more money.

As an initial matter, we must first realize that we are sick before we seek the assistance of a physician. And if we are already seeing a physician, but not getting well, then we must admit, to ourselves, that we are still hurting, not healing. That is the first step. There may be no recovery without that acceptance. It is easier for a mind that has accepted that things are not well to begin searching for effective ways to make things well. Lying that "it is well", when it is apparent that things are not well is bearing false witness, a violation of the Ten Commandments, a psychological method of sedating the mind not to spring into action. Sincere people should first fulfill their responsibilities before focusing on their rights. Righteousness, uprightness must precede "it shall be well." One is a "cause" and the other is a "consequence". We need to move into the arena of creative, innovative thinking, and verification if we are serious about bidding poverty goodbye forever and creating wealth. Time is of the essence. We are not going to live forever. Time to think, to act is running out. Let us be wise.

How does one bid poverty goodbye forever, develop the millionaire mindset, and begin to create wealth? Theoretically, the answer is easy. We need to format our minds, like I did, and download/develop new ideology/beliefs, like I am doing but very difficult practically. It takes time and patience. "The intellect has little to do on the road to discovery. There comes a leap in consciousness, call it intuition or what you will, and the solution comes to you and you don't know how or why." ~ **Albert Einstein**. "Creative thinking requires using the resources of the mind to come up with ideas that have not been thought of before. It requires knowledge, logic, imagination and intuition. To be considered creative, idea must not only be new, but must also be valued. Valued ideas are those that improve products, processes, or sense of well-being. To think creatively, one must, as a basic rule, want to have novel thought. Those who are firmly tied to prevailing thoughts may reject novel thoughts even if the thoughts jump into their minds." The Law of gravity states that "anything that goes up must come down." But in apparent contradiction to the law of gravity, the law of aerodynamics states that "it is possible for something to go up and remain there." And out of this paradigm shift in thinking came the birth of the flying machines. Create your own new thoughts today. Look for something that people say cannot be done. Think of it being done and think about how to do it. If you can do this, then your process to create wealth has begun. My own acts of creativity have commenced long ago. I have since broken the shackles of mental inertia. Now I soar in the realm of thoughts unhindered, yet aware of the consequences of negative and erroneous thoughts. And I have been handsomely rewarded with enhanced "sense of well-being." "Most of the important things in the world have been accomplished by people who have kept on trying when there seemed to be no hope at all." ~ **Dale Carnegie.**

Truth can be used to predict the future. If your own version of the truth is not predicting your future most of the time, you need to send it back to its manufacturer that is assuming you did not produce it yourself, for a repair, or for refund. Truth, undiluted, unslanted, untainted by delusion, can be used to predict the future, not just in some cases, but in most cases. Truth- upgrade your own version today. There are three tests of truth. One is the correspondence test. Let's say I received a bank alert for ₦100,000 yesterday. I did not know who sent it. And I did not tell anyone. And today, here you come, saying, did you get the alert for the ₦100,000 I sent you yesterday? That's an example of correspondence test. My experience corresponded with your utterance. Another test of truth is coherence test. Let's say someone comes to you. And after bragging of how blessed he is, how his prayers are always being answered, how he even had ₦200,000 in his account right now, he begs you to give him transport money to go home. Can you see that there is no coherence in his story? And consequently, the story, 9/10 cannot be true. Ah!!!! As someone who has developed a millionaire mindset, I love the third test of truth the most- the pragmatic test of truth. Let us say I tell you that I can play piano. Won't it be easy for you to know that I can truly play piano if you simply give me the piano to play for you to see? I think it will be. Once you see me playing the piano, my claim that I can play piano has not only pass the pragmatic test, it has also passed the correspondence and coherence tests. "Quench not the spirit, despise not prophecy. TEST all things..."

Bidding poverty goodbye forever and creating wealth must be based on clarity obtained from verification, and continuous striving to do the right things the right way, in all things, and at all times. It is a process, not a miracle. By becoming more competent and less corrupt, by having a sense of fairness, human dignity, and radiating love for humankind, you will conquer poverty on the short run and create wealth on the long run.

CHAPTER 2

DEVELOPING THE MILLIONAIRE MINDSET

"You will never get what you want, without knowing what it takes to get it." ~ **Brian Tracy.**

All things are created twice. The mental creation precedes the physical one. The same thing applies to bidding poverty goodbye forever and becoming a millionaire. You have to develop a millionaire mindset before you can become a millionaire. In order to develop a millionaire mindset, you have to be willing to make some changes in your life. Examine where you are. What do you need to do in order to become a millionaire? Do you need to change some friends that you are spending time with? Maybe you have outgrown them? Maybe they are not going to the land of wealth that is your next destination? You just may need to do just that. You have to break away from relationships that do not add to you. Make conscious effort to develop relationships with people who are going to your desired destination. Associate with people that inspire you to excel. Separate from people that hold you back emotionally and financially. Invest in your personal development to become the best that you can be. Goals, planning, commitment to the plan, and the planning process are very important to cultivating a millionaire mindset. You not only have to know where you are going, but you must also know how you are going to get there. A lot of things, including money-making ventures, never go exactly the way it is planned. You must develop the ability to keep on going when things are not going too well. This is what resiliency is all about.

A lot of people want to be millionaires. I know that you want to be one. That is why you are reading this book. You can become a millionaire if you meet or create great demand for a real service or product. You can become a millionaire by developing your human, social, and cultural capitals. "Human capital is the stock of knowledge, habits, social and personality attributes, including creativity, embodied in the ability to perform labor so as to produce economic value." And the factors that determine human capital are skills and knowledge, which include educational levels, work experience, social skills – communication, intelligence, emotional intelligence, personality – hard working, harmony in an office, habits, and personality traits, creativity and the ability to innovate new working practices/products.

The millionaire mindset requires excellence. "Excellence is a talent or quality which is unusually good and so surpasses ordinary standards. It is also used as a standard of performance as measured e.g. through economic indicators. Excellence is a continuously moving target that can be pursued through actions of integrity, being frontrunner in terms of products / services provided that are reliable and safe for the intended users, meeting all obligations and continuously learning and improving in all spheres to pursue the moving target." "Studies have shown that the most important way to achieve excellent performance in fields such as sport, music, professions and scholarships is to practice. Achievement of excellence in such fields commonly requires approximately 10 years of dedication, comprising about 10,000 hours of effort." The practice must be deliberate, with the objective of continuously improving in one chosen field.

Excellence is indeed a source of greatness. And excellence can be reached through the continuous refinement of innate talents, innate abilities, of which everyone possesses in one form or another. Therefore, go ahead; discover yourself, by yourself, for yourself. Go from ordinary to extraordinary. You've got it in you. Focus on yourself and your right doings instead of focusing on others and their wrongdoings. **Become the best you can be**. Continue to strive for excellence in all your doings. Go from incompetence, from mediocrity, to excellence, to transcendence.

A mere belief that you can become a millionaire alone does not mean you can. In order to develop a millionaire mindset, you have to become goal-orientated. You have to live within or below your means. You must convert your extra money to investment in your self-development or in other business ventures. Continuous learning is also a must for you. You also need to focus on how to make more money than you making right now. Learning how to create multiple streams of income and adopting smart savings habits is a must for you.

The rich and affluent cultivate mental makeup conducive to success. Their financial breakthroughs were not by magic. A lot of them came up with fresh ideas to solve real human problems. They were connected to the right people that made synergistic cooperation possible. Simply put, a major secret of millionaires is their ability to find solutions to the challenges of humanity. You have to do the same. Feeling connected to your friends and family, sharing your dreams with them, finding partners to do business with, engaging in your communities, finding solutions to perennial problems, overcoming challenges and making a difference are much more likely to happen when you build a strong network of quality relationships.

The following are some of the principles you must imbibe if you truly want to become a millionaire. Constantly visualize yourself as successful and as a millionaire. Study the management of business. Learn how to plan, organize, lead, and coordinate a business enterprise. Believe, without doubting yourself and your ability, that you will achieve success, and that you will become a millionaire. Build and surround yourself with a great network of people, mentors, influential friends, etc. Birds of a feather flock together. Working with people who already know the laws of success makes success easier to attain. I recommend finding people who have succeeded at your dream. Make them your mentors. Surround yourself with the smartest and most effective people you can find. You will never know everything. And you do not have to. But you must have someone within your network who knows what you need to know. Using the knowledge of others to accomplish your goals is using the power of other people. Harness your creativity. Be innovative: get creative when it comes to product ideas and overcoming obstacles. Make things happen and get things done. Make innovation a big thing. Use innovation to drive results and opportunities.

To be consistent is one of the vital ingredients in lasting success and enduring happiness. It is absolutely necessary for those who want to develop the millionaire mindset. Consistent means "acting or done in the same way over time, especially so as to be fair or accurate."

Lack of consistency is one of the factors of failure. Imagine that you have a car. Out of the seven days in a week, this car will only start and take you to work for three days. It will not start on the remaining four days. Your mechanic says there is nothing wrong with the car, that it is perfect. Is it? If anyone asks you about your car, will you say it is working well or there is something wrong with it? Whatever your answer is, use the same standard to measure your work or business ethics. Doing the right things the right way, in all things, and at all times, is a solid foundation for a solid work and ethics. Dedication and commitment to work, and constantly coming up with very good results is an example of strong work ethic.

While some people do only the barest minimum, or what is expected of them, someone with a millionaire mindset does more. He or she performs better. He goes the extra mile to come up with results that meet or exceed customers or employer's expectations. In business, quality is defined as meeting or exceeding customers' expectation. Going the extra mile is the action of rendering more and better service than that for which you are presently paid. When you go the extra mile, the Law of Compensation comes into play.

Someone with a millionaire mindset is disciplined. Discipline involves focus, dedication and determination on your part to do what you should. He or she is punctual. Punctuality is one of the first indicators of professionalism. Poverty loves procrastination. Whatever you have to do, do it promptly.

Being a critical thinker is one of the elements in developing a millionaire mindset. What is Critical Thinking? "Critical thinking is the ability to think clearly and rationally, understanding the logical connection between ideas." You must not only develop the ability to rigorously question ideas and assumptions rather than accepting them at face value, but you must also seek to determine whether the ideas, arguments and findings represent the entire picture. The ability to identify, analyze and solve problems systematically is very vital to development of the millionaire mindset.

Anyone with a millionaire mindset is also emotionally intelligent. And he/she is equally emotionally matured. He/she is fully aware of all his/her emotions. He/she understands them. He/she controls them instead of letting them to control him/her. And he/she expresses them via self-expression. Emotional Intelligence is the capacity to be aware of, control, express one's emotions, and to handle interpersonal relationships judiciously and empathetically. Emotional maturity is the ability to understand and manage one's emotions. Emotional intelligence is a key to both personal and professional success.

Having a millionaire mindset also requires financial intelligence. In order to start and run your own business profitably, you must understand basic accounting concepts. You must be able to read an income statement, a balance sheet, and a cash flow statement. You must know the difference between profitability and a healthy cash flow.

To become a millionaire, you need the right combination of powers. Without the right combination, you will suffer from "illusion of power". Becoming a multi-millionaire will be elusive. And, those without appropriate types of power blame external factors for their poverty. They may even believe that their family is cursed. Power, in all its meanings, is simply the ability to achieve. Possession of power makes most goals and objective achievable. To be without it is to sit back and wait until it is acquired. It may be delusional for one to brag about possessing power, and yet be unable to utilize it skillfully. Power of the mind precedes the manifestation of it externally. Develop it. Everyone has muscle. But not everyone is "cut up". Those with finely chiseled body, bulging biceps, and flat tummy have invested time in the gym, on the tracks, to arrive at that destination. They eat balanced diet that complement their rigors workouts. They simply followed a disciplined workout regimen. They nurtured what nature had provided for them. The same analogy can be applied to the human mind. Everyone has a mind. Not so? Call it brain if you will. I am now assuming that the mind houses the human intelligence. Therefore, the mind is akin to the control center, the determinant factor for the effective utilization of all the other human resources/talents. Without a sound mind, no matter how strong the body is the chance of becoming a load carrier at Oyingbo Market increases, the chance of being poor, high. The mind is the tool for acquiring knowledge, wisdom, and understanding. And these come through focused, disciplined study, observation, experimentation, verification, experience, intuition, creative thinking. Anyone interested in excellence, in leading, in living a fulfilling life devoid of problems, must learn how to do the right things the right way, in all things, and at all times.

Nature/God has already provided all the materials (input) we need to be successful, to be happy, and to continually add value to our society. However, we need to master ways and means (process) to turn these provided materials into desirable, favorable lives/products/services (output). Potential is not actual. But potential can be transformed into actual with the mastery of the input-process-output model. It is our duty and no one else to learn how to empower ourselves and break the chain of learned helplessness and generational classical conditioning.

Imagine a man that wants bulging muscles. He reads a book on how to develop muscles. He believes going to work out at the gym will work wonders. But he stops there. And he brags about his knowledge of muscle building. On the long run, a Mile 12 Market load carrier will have more muscles than him. During the course of my life, I have met many people who have mastered how to say the "right/good" things. But when it comes to performance, they either perform awfully, or do the complete opposite of their utterances. Also, I have met some people, albeit few, who do as they say, who practice what they preach, who "walk the talk", in small or big things, in good or bad things. These are authentic people, devoid of duplicity. If you want stability and trust in your business, in your life, seek them out. Cultivate them. Surround yourself with humans like these. These are the kind of people that sail my boat because they have integrity. Integrity, "the quality of being honest and having strong moral principles", is one of the most important ingredients of trust.

It may be easier to complain, to curse the darkness. But it is better, always, to light the candle to dispel the darkness. Lighting the candle is what someone with a millionaire mindset does. Complaining, criticizing, cursing is definitely easier to engage in. But seeking lasting solutions by doing the right things the right way, if not in all things, at least in most things, if not at all times, at least most of the time, may be more difficult, yet it provides the best solutions. Tokunbo Tonade literarily lit the candle instead of continuously complaining about the epileptic power supply in Nigeria. Tokunbo Tonade is the fifth of seven children born into the Victor Adekambi Tonade family of Ijeshatedo Isolo in Lagos State. The family lived their early lives in Sapele. This was a town in the old Bendel State, Midwest of Nigeria where they had to move westward to Lagos in the late 60s, away from the Nigerian civil war.

Tokunbo started his education in 1974 at Saint Paul's Anglican Primary School in Ijeshatedo, Isolo, Lagos. His secondary education was from 1979 to 1984 at Okota Grammar School also in Isolo, Lagos. After his secondary education, he was admitted into Opportunity Industrialization Center (OIC Pedro) Lagos where he obtained a Diploma in Auto Mechanics in 1987. After that, all his further education was self-taught. Majority of the learning was via the internet. All his self-tutoring was outside the four walls of formal education. He got married to Gbemisola Lawal on the 4th June 1999 and they have two boys.

Tokunbo Tonade carried out his industrial attachment at the Isolo workshop of BEWAC Motors Apapa in 1988 after which he proceeded as a floor mechanic to SCOA Motors at Ibara round-about in Abeokuta of Ogun State. From Abeokuta, he joined DAEWOO Motors Nig Ltd in Lagos as a supervisor mechanic which only lasted six months. He left DAEWOO Motors in November, 1991 to start his own automobile repair work shop called Tonad Motors at College Bus-stop in Isolo. The workshop was majorly into DAEWOO vehicle maintenance. He did this until 1996. He had clienteles ranging from numerous individuals to corporate bodies such as Honeywell, Ilupeju, Femstar & Company Ltd, Isolo, Academy Press, Ilupeju, and Rank Xerox, Matori, among others.

In 1997, Tonad Motors metamorphosed into Tonad Engineering. This was when he delved into the maintenance of diesel generators, design of automatic mains failures, design of control panel for small domestic generators and majorly into the construction of self-made diesel generators using vehicle engines. He succeeded in this venture so much so that he sold more than 50 units of this self-made diesel generators. As a result, he started making extra monies from the after sales services and routine maintenances all through to year 2001.

It was in 2001, an event occurred that changed the course of his life. This event brought about his venture into renewable energy which led to his two companies namely Concept Tech Enterprises and Fossildrag Ltd. During one of his periodic routine maintenance of the self-made generators for one of his clients, a dog died of carbon monoxide poisoning when it took shelter in the generator house on a stormy night. This particular dog happened to be the only one out of so many in his various clients' houses that actually never harassed or barked at him and he had grown very fond of the dog. It touched him quite deeply because he felt an overwhelming sense of responsibility for the dog's death, knowing his "self-made" generator inadvertently killed the dog.

This incident led him into researching "carbon monoxide poisoning" because he was hearing it for the first time then. During this research, he discovered that carbon emission did not only poisons living things but also poisons and depletes the ozone layer that protects the earth from the harmful rays of the sun and this had led to a phenomenal called global warming. After extensive research into global warming, he realized that the solution was to find and deploy a renewable source of energy to replace the present dependence on the use of fossil fuel worldwide. These discoveries made him stop further manufacturing of his self-made generators. This was his way of taking an affirmative action against global warming. The decision completely changed his preoccupation and his entire business model into providing renewable energy sources for electricity in order to replace the self-made diesel generators. It was at this point that the dream to build a house powered by solar was born. And so he founded and registered Concept Technologies in November 2002 to do precisely that.

As a result of this change in preoccupation and his self-education in solar energy, the workshop business nosedived so badly that he had to close shop. In order to feed his family, he took up work as a dredger maintenance engineer for IFL Dredging Ltd on Adeola Odeku Street in Victoria Island Lagos, where he was charged with the maintenance of a V12 floating dredger, the supervision of the company's 2.5 acre sand-fill which by extension also included a fifty feet sand pile and the running of three units of D6 bull dozers plus two pale-loaders. He did this until early 2003 when he resigned from IFL after realizing that he was convinced beyond any doubt of his new found passion for renewable energy. This was when the intense acquisition of relevant knowledge in renewable energy began on the internet. This went on for virtually two years with absolutely no tangible source of income while the family was being financially supported by his loving wife who now works for an advertising agency. After he felt he had known enough to string together a standalone solar installation, he started talking to some of his formal generator clients to give renewable energy a try. Majorities were not convinced but that did not discourage him as he kept advocating for cleaner energy sources relentlessly.

By late 2004, he was commissioned to install his first hybrid solar for a courier company called Express Partners at Oba Jobifele way, Alausa in Ikeja, Lagos. All the while through 2005, he was still doing some scanty diesel generator maintenance here and there to get by but kept his eyes on his passion for renewable energy. His second and third renewable energy job came 2006 in the form of inverter installation for Vetiva Capital Management's server room on Kofo Abayomi Strret in Victoria Island. The third was with Sahara Energy on Fowler Street in Ikoyi. And so on it went until an unexpected opportunity came to maintain GSM base stations and cell sites of then Zain Mobile, now Airtel. Things started looking up for him from then on. Right after then came along Ecobank who signed an SLA (service level agreement) that contracted Concept Technologies to maintain inverter back-up systems for their ATMs both in Lagos and southwest of Nigeria. It was while working for Ecobank that he was also approached by Skye Bank, now Polasis Bank Ltd to do a similar job for their ATM inverters and so another SLA was entered into with Skye Bank.

All the money that was made from the two banks was thrown into building his dream of a solar house and on the 3rd of September 2016, history was made when he completely disconnected the finally finished solar powered house from

PHCN. I was one of the invited guests, not only when he completely disconnected from Power Holding Company of Nigeria (PHCN), but also on 3rd of September, 2017, the one year anniversary of the disconnection. As at the time of this writing, the house has been running on solar for two years, powering all the appliances in the five bedroom bungalow which includes but not limited to a water pump, two fridges, one freezer, six units of one horse power air-conditioners and two bathroom water heaters. Tokunbo Tonade now has a new dream: to build an estate powered by solar using his second company by the name of Fossidrag Nig Ltd.

To bid poverty goodbye forever, it is very important to develop the millionaire mindset. Change what you cannot accept or tolerate. Accept or tolerate what you cannot change. This is a requirement for inner peace and joy. Trying to change, instead of accepting or tolerating what you do not have the power to change will produce pure grief. This is the hallmark of an emotionally balanced person. This is the hallmark of someone who has developed a millionaire mindset.

Develop the millionaire mindset and bid poverty away forever. Always be proactive."If you are proactive, you make things happen, instead of waiting for them to happen to you. Active means "doing something." The prefix pro- means "before." So if you are proactive, you are ready before something happens. The opposite is being reactive, or waiting for things to unfold before responding." ~ **Vocabulary.com dictionary**. William James wrote, "The greatest discovery of my generation is that a human being can alter his life by altering his attitudes of mind." Develop the millionaire mindset. It is your biggest asset. A mind that has developed the millionaire mindset is a generous mind. The possessor of that mind gives to those that are less fortunate. He or she has developed ability to focus for long period of time, the propensity for balanced and critical thinking, and the knack for quietly empowering others.

CHAPTER 3

DECISIONS DECIDE DESTINATION

"People do not decide their futures, they decide their habits and their habits decide their futures." ~ **F.M. Alexander.**

Poor decision- making is one of the factors that create poverty. In order to bid poverty goodbye forever, you have to learn how to make good decisions. A lot of problems can be prevented from the point of decision making. Henceforth, before making any decision, no exception, think well, analyze the facts, think critically and think creatively. Then decide firmly and implement effectively. Teach your children, if you have any, to do the same. It is dangerous not to teach our children how to think critically for themselves and how to analyze facts objectively.

Problem-solving and decision-making are important skills for you to have in not only your business, but also in your personal life. Problem-solving often involves decision-making. It is important to learn, to master the processes and techniques in order to improve your decision-making and, consequently, the quality of your decisions. Some people already find decision-making easy. So, these people should focus more on improving the quality of their decisions. However, some people are capable of making good decisions, but they always fail to act on the good decisions they have made. And, in doing so, they will fail to solve their problems effectively. Do not be like these people. Always act decisively on all your good decisions.

Problem-solving and decision-making are closely linked. And each requires creativity in identifying and developing options, for which the brainstorming technique is particularly useful. "Brainstorming is a group creativity technique by which efforts are made to find a conclusion for a specific problem by gathering a list of ideas spontaneously contributed by its members." ~ **Wikipedia.**

The first step in decision-making is to define and clarify the issue. The second step is to gather all the facts and understand their causes. The third is to think about or brainstorm possible options and solutions. The fourth step is to consider and compare the pros and cons of each option. The fifth is to select the best option. The sixth step is to explain the selected decision to those involved and affected, and follow up to ensure proper and effective implementation.

A lot of decisions have financial implications. Do not allow those that will not carry the financial burden attached to decisions to decide for you. Some of your decisions, your actions and inactions, in your attempt to cultivate the millionaire mindset, may not make sense to some people. And that is fine. But those decisions will make perfect sense to you and your pocket. After all, it is your pocket that has the final say, at this stage of your development, in what you should do or not do. In case you do not know, but I am sure you do, your pocket is what houses your money. With good decision making in money matters, you will no longer beg others for money. And, when you borrow money, make sure you only borrow to produce, to do business, never for consumption. Borrowing money to make more money is not the same as borrowing money for mere consumption. Borrowing money to make more money is a wise decision. Cutting your coat according to your fabric, not your size, must become your standard operating procedure. Make your financial burden very light, very affordable, and very liberating. Most of the time, if not all, you will feel blessed, not stressed.

Anyone that spends money faster than he makes it will always be broke. Anyone that does not cut his coat according to his fabrics will always beg, borrow or steal. I am talking about the type of stealing that is corruption. There is nothing beyond satisfaction but greed. Mitigate greed, and satisfaction will come easily. Then, contentment will be a constant companion. It is great when you can afford what you prefer. But, a lot of times, it is a good thing to prefer what you can afford. A person earning ₦35,000 per month, that is about $97 using about ₦360 to dollar exchange rate with a wife and two kids, did not cut his coat according to his fabrics. He may have, unwittingly, locked himself, and his family, into poverty. He is not practicing "doing the right things the right way", which is fundamental to lasting success and enduring happiness.

Agbada is nice. But I thought it was too expensive for me when I was still trying to save money for other necessities. I stuck with kaftan style, sans agbada. I told one of my friends this. And he said: "well, it is our tradition to wear agbada on special occasion like our children's wedding." I laughed hard. Tradition is "the transmission of customs or beliefs from generation to generation, or the fact of being passed on in this way." But when one of my daughters, Bolajoko Fayemi Odejayi, wedded in 2010, I did not wear agbada. And the Police did not come to arrest me. Did they? My decision was to save the money by not buying the extra five yards to sow agbada. I used the money saved to buy extra clothes. I love the feeling of not stressing over money, tradition or no tradition. After all, millionaires do not stress over money. Someone who has developed a millionaire mindset should also not stress over money because he is prudent in money management.

Imagine someone who does not have money. It is very obvious by the way he struggles to sustain himself. And, sometimes he has to beg others for money for food, transport, and rent. He is not content with his life. Neither is he fulfilled. And lately, his suffering and smiling has turned to suffering and frowning. Yet he believes he can spend money any way he wants because money is meant to be spent. Do I pity him? Or shall I say he deserves what he is getting, the obvious and the not so obvious one? After all, he holds the power to decide to be frugal in money matters. Inasmuch as I may empathize with why he or she made those decisions, I am more interested in the outcome, results, rewards that are consequential to those decisions. Some people make good decisions; while others make bad decisions. The most important thing is to have genuine reasons, relevant knowledge, for making your decisions. And ultimately, to have good results, rewards flowing from those decisions. You ought to know that decisions, effective or ineffective, are the building blocks to where we are heading, where we will be in the future. They are why we are where we are today. Most decisions have financial implications. Analyze the financial implications thoroughly before making any decision. Plans work more effectively when the money issues associated with the plans have been resolved. Make effective decisions. Seal that leak in your pocket. Save more. Invest more. Spend less. Those who call you selfish, stingy now will come and beg you for money later when your practical tips for making and keeping money catapult you to become a multi-millionaire.

If you are saving for your children's school fees and therefore unable to spend money for a celebration, are you stingy or frugal? If you are saving to invest more money to grow your business and therefore unwilling to give to someone who asks you for assistance to do the 10th year remembrance party for his late parents, are you frugal or stingy? To be frugal does not mean to be stingy. Frugal means "sparing or economical as regards money or food." Example: "I'm a bit too frugal to splash out on designer clothes" Synonyms of frugal are: thrifty, sparing, economical, saving, etc. To be stingy is to be "mean; ungenerous." Anyone, I repeat, anyone who is not frugal with his or her meager resources will end up begging others for money or other things of value. Calling those who may be prudent in money matters "stingy" is nothing but emotional manipulation. I honestly think it takes a beggar to know the stingy. I knew someone that squandered his resources on musicians when the going was good. But when he ran broke and got sick, those he begged for medicine money did not come to his aid. But when he died from the sickness, they contributed money to give him "a befitting burial", whatever that means.

Wealth can be generational. And so is poverty. Not having fabrics at all may be as a cumulative consequence of not cutting one's coat according to one's fabrics in the first place. All the money that has been spent on those needless, ceaseless, avoidable celebrations could have been either saved or invested in profitable ventures. Never spend money you have not received. Do not promise someone money based on a promise you have from someone else. It is better late than never, to start putting to more productive use, that money being spent on those needless, ceaseless, avoidable celebrations. Stop locking yourself into poverty. It is better to be prudent in money matters. It is better to invest, to save for rainy days. And it always rains. Profligate people pay a stiff price on the long run. I know because I have been both. This is real talk, not book talk: being there, done that. As an adult, no one is responsible for your welfare but yourself. As you lay your bed in your youth, so you will lie on it in your old age. I read the following story written by Crownson on Nairaland, but it was said to be originally written by Ronald Nzimora.

"I once read a fascinating story about lobsters. You know what lobsters are right? Those giant crayfish-like looking sea "animals" people like to eat. How does anyone eat seafood? They give me an allergic reaction! Anyway, so here's the story: when waves roll and crash against the rocks, they will carry with it tens of these lobsters and when the waves roll back, the lobsters are left behind. A lobster when left high and dry among the rocks does not have the instinct and energy enough to work its way back to the sea, so it waits for the sea to come to it and take it back. Sometimes though the sea never comes back to roll over those rocks on which the lobsters are. If the sea does not come, the lobster within a yard of the waves remains where it is and dies. Why would it do this? Why would it choose to die although it could have prevented its own death if only it would make the slightest effort to reach the waves that are just beyond those rocks? Turns out this is a valuable lesson for you and I because, guess what? The world is full of human lobsters, people who sit and wait for permission to start living their best life. People who are waiting for the perfect time, the perfect conditions, the perfect tools, the perfect amount of money, before they get off their hiney and do something to change their station in life. Men and women stranded on the rocks of indecision, self-doubt and procrastination, who, instead of putting forth their own energies, are waiting for some grand wind of good fortune to blow them into the sea and set them afloat. They are the people who are waiting to "hammer", waiting to be handed things, waiting for things to be done for them. So they wait and wait and wait, like Godot, forever, when they could simply have reached out and taken everything they could ever want. I don't want this to be you. Please don't be a human lobster."

I truly think that life is complex, not easy. But the complexity of life can be simplified by our intelligence, our thinking, our behavior. Adequate knowledge and superb foresight are some of the quintessential for making effective life-simplifying decisions that prevent, solve vexing problems.

Our values are the things that we believe are important in our lives. They determine our priorities. Or they ought to. When the things that we do and the way we behave match our values, life is usually good. We are satisfied and content. We are happy and fulfilled. The real source of unhappiness is when these do not align with our values. This is why making a conscious effort to identify our values is so important. Life is easier when you acknowledge your values and make plans and decisions that honor them. If you are unhappy, revisit your values. When you make decisions and act contrary to your values, you will be unsatisfied and unhappy on the long run. Our decisions may determine our destinations, but it is our values that determine our decisions, most of the time. Therefore, make sure you have the values that you will enjoy their intended or unintended consequences.

When we lack the resources to acquire certain basic necessities of life, we do one of these six things:

(1) We do without. (2) We become parasitic in our thinking and behavior. (3)We beg. (4) We acquire through corruption. (5) We abandon to God and resign to fate. (6) We try to find the reason to why we lack required resources in the first place, and then come up with creative solutions to the problems.

Some of us use a combination of these methods at the same time. I personally have used all the methods during the course of my life. And the one that has the highest value to me because of who I am is number six (6). If you are like me, try to find the reasons to why you lack required resources in the first place. And then come up with creative solutions to your problems. Initial tools needed: clarity of mind. Sincerity of heart.

Cut your coat according to your fabrics. The fewer things you want, the easier you can get them and the happier you will be. The more you are content with what you have, the more satisfaction and happiness you will get. By simply contracting my appetite, and distending my scruples, I am now the happiest and the most contented man. It is very possible to be comfortable in life without flamboyance, without extravagance.

Also imagine the story of a married woman. She was given

₦200,000 to pay for her children's holiday lessons. She bought hair extensions instead. Then, she sent her children to a friend's house garden to play during the day. Her husband had no idea what was going on until a family friend saw the children twice at the garden. He confronted her but she vehemently denied it. How on earth does a woman prefer hair extensions to bettering her children's life? Is this not the case of ruination of a nation starting from the household?

For now, you may be working for money. However, your goal is to have money working for you. Work to build assets. Assets make money. That money then buys more assets. That money will then be working for you. Your money, through buying cash-flowing assets, will be making you more money. That is how to become financially free. This means that "you get to make life decisions without being overly stressed about the financial impact because you are prepared. You control your finances instead of being controlled by them." Are your decisions leading you towards financial freedom or away from it? Do you have money saved up for rainy days? Do you invest a portion of your salary? Do you have effective money management skills? Do you want to start and manage your own business?

CHAPTER 4
TIME IS MONEY

"No such thing as spare time. No such thing as free time. No such thing as down time. All you got is life time. Go!" ~ **Henry Rollins - Actor -Musician.**

Are you using your time wisely? Are you investing it in activities that, not only enhance your mental growth, mental development, but also your future earnings? Or are you majorly investing it in activities that neither have mental development capability, nor have future earnings potentials?

Time is one of the vital variables in making money. Money is a store of value that is used as a medium of exchange. Time is indeed money: It is your greatest asset. And, fortunately, it is also a variable that we all have equal amount. However, how and where we use our time ultimately determines how much money we will make.

Early in life, we are all sent to one school or the other. Without our knowing why, someone in our lives was making sure we invest our time in developing our human capitals. "Human capital is a collection of traits – all the knowledge, talents, skills, abilities, experience, intelligence, training, judgment, and wisdom possessed individually and collectively by individuals in a population. These resources are the total capacity of the people that represents a form of wealth which can be directed to accomplish the goals of the nation or state or a portion thereof." The backbone of our human and economic growth is the development of our human capital early in life. The more time we invest in our education and experience, the more our human capital increases. While investing time in developing and increasing our human capital, we are also, wittingly or unwittingly, developing our social capital. Even though social capital can be defined in different ways, it is basically the same meaning. It is simply the resources built up through connections or relationships among people.

Social capital is "the networks of relationships among people who live and work in a particular society, enabling that society to function effectively." It "Consists of the economic resources garnered from human interactions. The resources include those of tangible and non-tangible assets, such as information, innovative ideas, and financial support." Social capital is as valuable as financial capital. The wise investment of time in developing human and social capitals will ultimate bring in the money. It is just a matter of time.

How valuable is your time to you and others? The more time you have invested in human capital development, the more valuable your time is, not only to you, but also to others. Please invest your time wisely. Always be passionate about getting pertinent knowledge and acquiring useful skills. Invest your time and money to get them. It may not be easy, but it is imperative to spend your money on these types of assets. They will put money back into your pocket on the long run. Yes, other people are not just going to pay for your time, they are going to pay for what you are capable of doing with the time. Those things you focus on, the ones you invest your time in, are the things that will eventually form your habits. They are the things you are likely going to be good at doing. So, make sure that those things have more economic values than the recreational ones.

In the beginning of your journey to create wealth, all you have may be your time. You may sell this time by working for others. And, you save a chunk of what you are paid for your time. This will be used as investments. However, to transcend, to create wealth, you have to be able to pay other people to use their time for you.

Wasting time on frivolity is a contributor to poverty. Imagine a lady that constantly parties while her friend goes to work. Who may turn around to beg the other for money to do hair, to do nails? Also imagine a man that is constantly drinking in bars while his friend goes out to learn a trade. Who may turn around to beg others for money to eat, to hang out with the fellas? Those who use their time wisely earn their money legitimately, and save it prudently. These are the people that some of society's beggars term stingy. I sincerely sympathize, empathize with them. The unfair ones are those who fritter their time away on frivolities, who fritter their income away on ceaseless, avoidable celebrations, then turn around to beg for sustenance, for emergencies. Always remember that what we mostly cannot do presently is because of what we did not do in the past, but ought to have done. Poverty loves procrastination. Whatever you have to do, do it promptly. Time is money. Time is precious. The productive use of your time is essential to not just your success, but also to your happiness.

CHAPTER 5
SAVINGS

"Often, the blame for our pain rests on the simple choices we make every day." ~ **David Westerdahl.**

If you lose your income today, do you have enough money saved to last you for, say, six months? The money we receive as salary, for rendering a service, or return on our investments is called income. A portion of our income that is not to be spent on consumption is called savings. Savings can fill in the gap between loss of income and poverty, until another source of income is found. Most income earners are mostly one paycheck away from poverty. Poverty is real. Protect yourself with sound financial knowledge and practice. Be prudent in money matters. You may need to cut off those expenses that are preventing you from savings. Saving money requires self-discipline.

To secure our financial future, we must not only save, we must also invest. If you are not doing any of these, the best time to start is now. This of course will require changes in how you spend money. A general rule of thumb is said to be that we should save for short term and invest for long term. Banks provide a safe place for you to save your money. Banks' checking and savings accounts offer you liquidity and flexibility.

No matter how small you think your income is, you can still save money if you are determined, and disciplined. When I started working as a personnel clerk at Nigeria Airways in 1978, my salary was one hundred naira a month. And, in a span of two years, I was able to save one thousand naira. I eventually used the one thousand naira to purchase $1, 800 BTA (Basic Traveling Allowance), which I took with me to Forth-Worth, Texas, in search of personal growth and development. Yes, one thousand naira was one thousand and eight hundred dollars when I first travelled out in 1980. Therefore, sometimes, it is not so much of how little money we are making, but how well we are managing that money.

Many people find it tough to save money. It is easier to spend money than to make it. There are many reasons why this is so. And one of that reasons is that our expenses are higher than our income. Sometimes, there are genuine reasons why expenses will rise even though income is stagnant. With a budget, you figure out what your income is and what your expenses are. Once you know these two things, you can look for ways to reduce your expenses or increase your income to allocate an amount of money that you can afford to save.

A lot of people say they do not have enough money. But you have to increase your ability to earn if you want to increase your income. You can do that by increasing the value you add to your society. To add more value to your society, "Learn a new skill, do the work no one else is willing to do and say yes to more of the right things and no to more of the wrong things. Focus on the few tasks that bring the most value to the world and outsource the rest."

Prudence in money matters is a quintessential in sustainable happiness. "According to the "50/30/20 Rule", you should put 20 percent of your income into savings. Another 50 percent should be spent on necessities (rent, food, utilities, health insurance), with 30 percent devoted to discretionary expenses, like travel, cable TV, eating out, movie tickets, etc. Additionally, you should have enough saved to sustain you for six months, should you lose your job or fall ill and be unable to work. Some argue that it's best to cap this at a year..." Let us imagine that your income is ₦100,000 a month, take 20% of that, which is ₦20,000, consider it as saving, and put it in the bank. ₦50,000, which is 50%, is the amount to be spent on necessities (rent, food, utilities, airtime credit etc. The remaining 30%, which is ₦30,000, is the amount you will devote to discretionary expenses, like travel, eating out, movie tickets, etc.

A lot of people have no financial skills. They have no idea how best to use their money. They live impulsively, reacting to life around them, allowing society to decide how best to spend their money. I see people, a lot of people, struggling to put a 20kg financial load on a stand designed to carry a 10kg load. Of course they are not stupid people. They are only trying to follow the dictates of their religion or their culture. But if they simply put a 10kg financial load on a stand designed to carry a 10kg load, they will stay afloat, even in troubling times.

When you are starting out in life, saving money is very vital. I learned that very early in life. If you cannot save your money then the chances of you becoming a millionaire later on drop drastically or almost disappear. Even if you just start by saving a little money right now this is better than saving none at all. Start somewhere and start soon. The money you saved will eventually save you when opportunities come or emergency emanates.

How can one save money that is not enough? By first changing some habits that drain one's purse. The bad spending habit we have created is a product of our thinking and behavior. It cannot be changed without changing our thinking and our behavior. Regardless of your income, consistently spend less than you make.

Discipline is essential to savings. Without discipline, it is difficult to do the right things the right way. It is difficult to put some money away for rainy days when there is immediate need for it. However, becoming self-disciplined is imperative to those who want to save, who always want to enjoy the simple pleasures of life. It is almost impossible to enjoy the simple pleasures of life without money.

For a lot of people, their income is not enough. And if they take out 20% of it to save, the income will still not be enough. However, if they are disciplined to keep saving that 20% of their inadequate income, it will eventually accumulate. That accumulation of funds can then be used as seed money, as a step up the ladder of success, away from pervasive poverty. This clearly shows why saving ought to be a very high priority for those who want to escape from poverty.

Your savings should not only be for major purchases, it must also be for emergency and retirement. If your wife is pregnant, you have nine months to save for any eventuality. Giving birth through a C-section is not an unforeseen circumstance. Proper planning prevents poor performance. And what is so unforeseen about old age? Everyone will attain it if we live long enough.

Health does fail sometimes. And when health fails, it not only prevents us from making money, it also saps our savings and the savings of our loved ones. This is even truer for those of us living in countries without governmental medical assistance. I think this is one reason to have emergency savings. Most of the money we plough into all those ceaseless celebrations we engage in can be saved for the day our health might fail. The occasional failing of health is a foreseen circumstance to the circumspect citizens.

I knew a man who had inadequate money to begin with. He was underemployed. Yet he took his inadequate money and he squandered it on cultural/religious celebrations. He sprayed his already inadequate money at parties just to impress people that he had money. And when he was broke,--and he was always broke--he begged others for money. Anyone that did not give according to his whim was labeled stingy. I eventually told him the same story I told in chapter 3: I knew someone that squandered his resources on musicians when the going was good. But when he ran broke and got sick, those he begged for medicine money did not come to his aid. But when he died from the sickness, they contributed money to give him "a befitting burial", whatever that means. It is better to be prudent in money matters. It is better to invest, to save for rainy days. And it always rain. Profligate people pay a stiff price on the long run. I know because I have been both. This is real talk, not book talk: being there, done that. As an adult, no one is responsible for your welfare but yourself. As you lay your bed in your youth, so you will lay on it in your old age.

The experience I am sharing here is to showcase the link between saving money and becoming a millionaire. This incident happened in 1985. I had been living in Nigeria for a little over two years, after the completion of my flight training in Texas United States. Ultimately, frustration drove me from Nigeria, as a trained pilot. It drove me to the street of Staten Island, New York, broke. I had only two shirts and two trousers, with fifty cents in my pocket. I used forty cents out of the fifty to call my brother, Niyi, to pick me up from JFK Airport. He took me to Staten Island so I could spend some days with him before traveling to Texas, to work in the factory, like I had done during my flight training days. The next day, I followed him to work. He was working as a gypsy taxi driver. It was then I realized that driving taxi was an easier and more lucrative job than the factory one waiting for me in Texas. I made my choice. Niyi introduced me to one Willie Bernard. Willie Bernard was originally from Liberia. He worked in corporate America and he had all sorts of credit cards. Willie rented a car for me. And I became a gypsy taxi driver. I was working for about eighteen hours a day. I began to make money. And I needed to save it. So, I went to Citibank on Bay Street Staten Island, New York with my earnings. I wanted to open a checking account. But the bank manager refused to open it for me. Why? Because I had a green passport. We were already notorious for bank fraud. I was angry. I was being punished for a crime I had not committed. I told the bank manager that all I needed was a place to keep my money. So he opened a savings account for me. And I began to save a minimum of $30 everyday. Within six months, I had about $8, 000 in that savings account. Shortly after that, the same bank manager that would not open a checking account for me six months before, called me to his office, opened a checking account for me, filled a form for a Visa credit card and overdraft for me, asked me to sign the computer generated forms and not the usual forms that people filled to apply for credit cards and bank overdraft. Within six weeks, my Citibank Visa credit card and the approval for bank overdraft came in the mail. And I was ready to launch my career as a businessman. I already had the vital tools. With the credit card, and a valid New York State driver's license, I was able to rent luxury cars from the car rental companies, and re-rent them, at a very high price, for those who want to rent cars, but without credit cards. Someone later said I was at the right place at the right time. He failed to see the deeds that produced the results.

So, when someone said, "white people don't give black people credit in America", I surreptitiously looked at my skin color, to check if I was still black. I already knew that my bank manager was white. For the above statement to be true, I must also be white to have acquired those credits. But I knew I was not. Therefore, that statement was not true. And just like Jimmy Cliff sang, "you can get it if you really want. But you must try, try and try. You'll succeed at last..." Get rid of your self-imposed limitations. You may be able to do what others had told you cannot be done. It may be true that they cannot do it. But you may be able to do it. Let your inner self be your guide. Is it telling you that you can do it? Do not give up and never quit. Never allow temporary setback to beat you down. Keep going no matter what get in your way. Obstacles, to someone with a millionaire mindset, are no more than another challenge. But be careful not to acquire expensive hobbies and lifestyles which can be a huge drag on your financial resources. "He who takes advice about his savings from one, who is inexperienced in such matters, will pay with his savings for proving the falsity of their opinions."

"Make at least a penny more than you spend. If you make a penny less, you are out of business." Simply put, this warning is saying you should spend less than you make, and not more. But in my youthful years, I was oblivious to this warning. The act of admitting our mistakes can lead to powerful, pertinent changes we so desired. My bad habits made me deaf. Gambling was one of my bad habits. It was my Achilles Heels. Sometimes in 1992, my daughter's mom, my daughter, Ayodele, and I came to Nigeria for a visit. Few days before we travel back to New York, I decided to go and buy our traveling tickets. On passing through Allen Avenue in Ikeja, I saw some of my friends cars parked in front of another friend's office. I smiled. I knew what they were doing. I told my driver to park, and I went in. From about 1:00pm, we gambled until about 11:30pm. All my money for our tickets was lost on the gambling table. Who wanted to buy my car? The winner at the gambling table accepted the offer and gambling resumed in earnest. The next day was Saturday. There was environmental sanitation, so no movement until 10:00am. A taxi was called to take me home at 10:00am, sans a kobo. My driver asked me where my car was and I told him to shut up. I asked him if the car was mine or his. The following year, 1993, I came back to Nigeria from New York. This time, I came alone. And I purposely stayed at Eko Merridian Hotel on Victoria Island, Lagos simply because the hotel had a casino in-house. I lost so much money and it scared me. I suddenly realized that I had lost control and no longer had the will power to stop gambling. Addiction had taken over my reasoning capability. I had prayed to no avail. So a friend recommended a visit to a fix-it-all babalawo, a Yoruba name for a native doctor. Even though I did not believe in that type of thing, I agreed to go because I had lost control over myself, over my thinking faculty. The place was in Ota, Ogun State. The dazzling began. A bath in the nearby flowing stream, Oro came out during the day; Olodumare was called upon, all on my behalf. Confidently, the babalawo proclaimed that I would never gamble again. Weak will power looking for solace made me to believe him. The same night, I lost twice the amount I had lost prior to the Ota visit. The trek on the path of addiction, towards ruination continued. Finally, in 1996, I quit gambling. The gap between deciding to quit and the actual quitting was a full year. That was how strong the clutch gambling had on me, on my mind. Gambling thrills, yes, but it is addictive. And it can ruin someone's life. It will definitely prevent one from saving, from building the famous egg nest that's necessary for growth, for retirement. There are two costs for every purchase or expenditure you make. The first price is the actual price you pay for the purchased item. The second price is the price you pay to forgo the alternative use for your money. The opportunity cost for gambling away millions of Naira is money-making business I did not set up.

You are in control of your financial future. The universe does not care if you suffer or not. The responsibility for not suffering rests on your shoulder. The purpose of money is to provide comfort and pleasure for you and your loved ones. That makes understanding money, making it, and spending it very important. Good spending habits might be a tough call at first, but they produce a lifetime of rewards. Form a saving habit. Save some money every day, even if it is a little. Saving money is difficult, while spending in an undisciplined way is gratifying. But if you want to retire comfortably, you must save part of your income consistently for several decades.

If the reason for wearing a wrist watch is to know what the time says, why wear one when I already have two phones telling me what the time is? Wristwatch, for me, has become a relic of the past, and therefore, redundant. My constant companions, my phones, perform the exact function a wristwatch performs for me: they are stylish, elegant, and they tell me the time. So, why waste more money to buy a new wristwatch when the old ones have become antics, mere decoration for my cupboard? I have simply stopped wearing wrist watches. And anytime I have the urge to buy a stylish wristwatch, I simply convert the money to my retirement savings. That is just it.

The more fulfilling activities you engage in, the more money you are going to spend, and the less disposable income you are going to have. Well, that may not be a bad thing if the fulfilling activities are largely economic activities that will yield future returns. But if they are largely social activities without significant financial returns, that may not be too good on the long run. Is this not the reason why a lot of people beg for money instead of cutting their coat according to their fabrics or out rightly doing without? Some of us have learned how to shrink our social obligations to a manageable proportion that our pocket can accommodate. But the majority has not. They want to keep on doing as it has always been done, even if they have to transfer the financial burden to other people, because they cannot afford it. Change is beckoning to them. They ought to answer the voice of change.

Sometimes in 2014, I went to pay someone a visit. He asked me if I wanted a Coke. I said yes. So, he gave me a bottle of plastic Coke. "Don't you have the bottled one?" I asked. He did not. Too bad. I kind of preferred the taste of the bottled one. And it was cheaper. "Why do you buy plastic Coke instead of the bottled one?" He had no tangible reason. He was just going with the flow, reacting, like the majority, instead of acting based on critical, reasonable analysis. That was when I lectured him on how he would save fifty Naira every time he bought a 50cl bottled Coke instead a 50cl plastic Coke. Plastic Coke cost ₦120 in his neighborhood while the bottled one cost ₦70. Same product but in different container. Why pay ₦50 for a plastic he would, could not eat but throw away? Ego trip? Just imagine how much he could save by applying this concept to all his other spending. It has been said that a penny saved is a penny earned. And the two known ways to have more money is either to make more or spend less. Hope you can see how, and why, you have to begin to cut your coat according to your fabrics. This can be done without sacrificing satisfaction, fulfillment, and enjoying the simple pleasures of life.

The paradox about money is that we want wealth so that we can spend money freely. However, creating wealth demands that we do not spend money freely in the beginning. Because wealth is not so easy to create, we have to spend with sense if we want to accumulate, create wealth.

CHAPTER 6
INVESTING

In chapter 5, you read about savings, which is essentially for your short term needs. We save for purchases and emergencies. We save for things that need a vehicle to sit in, available when we need them and have low risk of losing value. This part deals with investing a portion of your savings for your long term needs. The key difference in saving and investing is that, while savings is to keep our money safe, making very little return, investing is to make money for us. However, as good as savings is, savings alone cannot make you rich. One of the reasons for saving money is to invest. The way to get rich is to make investments in projects you are knowledgeable about. It is much easier to lose money than to gain it.

One of the most effective ways to earn more money over time is investing it, and the earlier you start the better. You can make more money if you invest it correctly. Therefore, be committed to investing and make your money grow. You know how hard you worked for your money. Do not be too quick to part with it. Constantly update your knowledge by continuous learning. Business is about risk-taking. Be prepared to take calculated risk.

Saving is a vital part of personal finance. Its purpose is to protect and provide for our future. Savings is to protect against an uncertain future. It is also to help us fulfill our dreams. Savings helps us pay for emergency. It provides funds for us in case we lose our job. However, many people stop at saving. Savings is like a seed that has to be planted. Do not just keep the seed. Plant it into different types of investment vehicles that will grow your savings. You can also put the money in a business, if you are an entrepreneur. However, be warned that you can easily lose your money in business if you are not too careful.

Savings includes putting money into a savings account like a money market or Certificate of Deposit (or CD). It has little risk of loss of funds but also has minimal gains. You are able to pull money out of your savings when you want (or after a period of time) to use. But when you invest, you have the potential of better gains or rewards, long term, but also the potential for loss. Savings, as it has been said, is not an end in and of itself. We accumulate savings so we can do the things we want to do. We use savings to buy assets. Assets put money in our pocket. A properly run rental house is an asset that will put money in your pockets.

There are various types of investments that can help you achieve your financial goals.

A certificate of deposit is savings tool. This tool is relatively short term, ranging from a few months to many years. While in the CD, your money is safe and grows at a little bigger interest rate, than in a regular savings account but you do not have access to it until the term of the CD is over.

"What is a Stock or Share? When you buy a stock, you are buying a piece of the company. When a company needs to raise money, it issues shares. This is done through an initial public offering (IPO), in which the price of shares is set based how much the company is estimated to be worth, and how many shares are being issued. The company gets to keep the money raised to grow its business, while the shares (also called stocks) continue to trade on an exchange, such as the Nigerian Exchange and the New York Stock Exchange (NYSE) for example. Traders and investors continue to buy and sell the stock of the company on the exchange, although the company itself no longer receives any money from this type of trading. The company only receives money from the IPO." "Traders and investors continue to trade a company's stock after the IPO because the perceived value of company changes over time. Investors can make or lose money depending on whether their perceptions are in agreement with "the market." The market is the vast array of investors and traders who buy and sell the stock, pushing the price up or down."

"The ultimate goal of buying shares is to make money by buying stocks in companies you expect to do well, those whose perceived value (in the form of the share price) will rise." "Mature and established companies may also pay a dividend to shareholders. A dividend is a cut of the company's profit, which the company sends to shareholders as long as the company continues to pay the dividend." ~ **Investopedia.**

A bond is a loan an investor makes to an organization in exchange for interest payments over a specified term plus repayment of principal at the bond's maturity date. Learn how corporate, muni, agency, treasury and other types of bonds work. Bond is unlike stock: when you buy shares of a company's stock, you own a piece of that company. Stocks come in a wide variety, and they often are described based on the company's size, type, performance during market cycles and potential for short- and long-term growth. Learn more about your choices—from penny-stocks to large caps and more.

Treasury bills have higher rate than fixed deposits. And they are more stable. Treasury bills are issued by a country's central bank. But you can purchase them through your local bank by giving them instruction. The rate is normally higher than fixed deposits. You may get your interest upfront, meaning that your interest for one year is paid at the point of purchase or at the end of each payment quarter.

Money market fund is an open-ended mutual fund that deals in short-term discount securities such as treasury notes, bank bills and promissory notes. The money market funds are managed by experienced funds managers who are trained to optimize shareholder returns by deploying a balance mix of portfolio investing to ensure the investor's money is safe and returns remain higher than the inflation rate.

A lot of People have been sucked into various ponzi schemes just to make quick money to augment their purchasing power. About two years ago, I visited New Garage, Ibadan, the capital of Oyo state in Nigeria. I saw a large crowd in front of a shopping plaza. The crowd was shouting and wailing: "Chibuzor has run away o. All these people's money has disappeared into thin air."

Chibuzor promised to pay ₦25,000 for every ₦10,000 brought to him as investment. He rented an office, employed few locals who manned the office. He also employed beautiful ladies who went out to solicit funds for the money doubling scheme. The gullible brought in money. Chibuzor got rich. Then he failed to fulfill his promise to pay. Petition was written. SARS came. Arrests were made. But Chibuzor got away. He may resurface in another neighborhood.

The next day, a lady surfaced. That day was the day her ₦40,000 investment ought to be ripe for the collection of ₦100,000. I knew she had plans of how she would spend her windfall from the money doubling scheme. But when she arrived at the Ibadan New Garage office of the money doubling magnate, she met the place under lock and keys. What was going on? She was told the news of the petition, the arrests by SARS, and all. She was told the Chibuzor has fled from Ibadan. She mentioned "elubo money" before she fainted. I left before she was revived.

I went back the next day to get more gists. Chibuzor was still nowhere to be found. But he would not be going back to Onitsha where he came from. Why? A lot of people in Onitsha were looking for him also, for taking their money and failing to pay the promised 150%. Some of the locals that Chibuzor employed as sales agents were also in hiding. I heard some people leaving threatening words at the scene of the crime. I heard "tyre". I heard "petrol". I also heard "matches." I thereafter left the scene, with no plans of going back.

It is also wise to understand the current foreign exchange rate and its propensity for fluctuation before investing. Let us say, in September of 2015, I took $2500 out of my domiciliary account and changed it to naira at the rate of ₦200 to $1, which came to ₦500,000. The money was used to execute a business with a 50% profit margin. The infamous Nigerian factor kicked in.

Payment was delayed. But the capital and the profit came in intact, albeit about a year late. Now, fast forward to October, 2016. I decided to change the money and return it to the domiciliary account it came from. The whole money, capital plus profit totaling ₦740,000 were exchanged for $1,610. The rate of exchange on that day was ₦460 to $1. That was a loss of about $900.

Investing can be risky and full of uncertainty. Do not invest your hard earned money in some risky investments with propensity for high returns as an avenue to make money without consulting a professional in finance. In business matters, be wary of those who ignore facts and figures when formulating economic ideas. Not only will they throw their own money away, they will make yours too depart from you. Scan your environment; gather your facts and figure, then, create your strategic plan for all your economic activities.

Lastly, let us assume that your house needed painting. But you could not afford it yet because you had to pay your children's school fees. Let us assume, again, that one day, you were coming back from work and you met painters painting your house. Instead of querying them to find out why they were painting your house, who sent them, who would pay etc, you greeted them, and quietly went inside, happy at the miraculous work of God in your life. The following morning you received the bill for the house painting. Of course you refused to pay because you were not the one who asked the painter to paint your house. Were you right?

The true picture was: the painter made a mistake. The owner of house number 18 asked the painters to paint his house. But because of miscomprehension, the painter came to your house, which was number 8. It was an honest mistake that you could have corrected when you saw the painters painting your house. When the case got to court because you did not pay the bill, the court ruled against you. According to the court, the rule of contract had two elements: Offer and Acceptance. The court construed the painting of your house as "Offer" from the painters. It went on to construe your quietly going inside your house on the day of the incident as "Acceptance". Would you appeal or accept the court's verdict? Before wasting your hard earned money on appeal, you need to know what an 'Implied Contract' is. What is an 'Implied Contract ' An implied contract is an agreement created by actions of the parties involved, but it is not written or spoken. An implied contract is a legal substitute for a contract that is assumed to have been drawn. In this case, there is neither written record nor any actual verbal agreement. By letting your expenses to exceed your income, by not saving and investing as you should, you are unwittingly accepting the offer of poverty with your behavior. By developing the millionaire mindset, by being prudent in money matter, you are wittingly accepting the offer of wealth with your behavior. The choice is yours. Choose wisely.

CHAPTER 7
ASSOCIATE WITH LIKE MIND/LAW OF ATTRACTION

Magnet attracts metal but not plastic. Who you are, the substance you are made of, your thoughts/beliefs, knowledge and skills decide what you attract into your life. Once you have developed your human capital, you unavoidably attract like minds to yourself. Success does not come without the cooperation of others. Success attracts more success while failure attracts more failure.

You ought to learn to network to meet the right people. This is to develop your social capital."Social capital can be defined as the resources built up through connections or relationships among people." Are your present connections and relationships plus or minus? Do you have the same values? Do you have similar goals and ambition with your circle of friends? Are your friends contributing to your goals and dreams? Do you have the type of friends that all you guys do together is spending money but not making money? Your circle of friends should not be about just social activities. The circle should also be about economic activities. You and your friends can still gossip, have fun and create wealth at the same time. Unity of value, of purpose, synergy and equal power. And power is the ability to achieve. This is what your social capital ought to be used for. As human beings, we have the ability to bring into our lives that which we focus on. Law of attraction uses the power of the mind to translate whatever is in our thoughts into concrete reality.

Rich people have rich friends. And poor people have poor friends. But knowledgeable, skillful, and diligent people can mingle with the rich and the poor. This is the main reason why developing you human capital is of vital importance. The following is a pertinent explanation by one Swami Vivekananda of the meaning of 'Association'. He is reported to have said: "A rain drop from the sky: if it is caught by clean hands, is pure enough for drinking. If it falls in the gutter, its value drops so much that it cannot be used even for washing your feet. If it falls on a hot surface, it will evaporate... If it falls on a lotus leaf, it shines like a pearl and finally, if it falls on an oyster, it becomes a pearl... The drop is the same, but its existence and worth depends on whom it is associated with."... Always be associated with people who have the same values, goals and ambition as you.

Some people were not fed excellence when they were young. So, naturally, they did not grow up with the knowledge of what it tasted like, not to talk of how to produce it. They were fed mediocrity, frivolity. So, naturally, they recognize the taste of these. And they gravitate towards them, just like metals gravitate towards a magnet. However, mediocrity and frivolity are natural enemies of success, of happiness. They are not conducive for growth, for progress. You need to get rid of them if you are serious about creating wealth.

We like people that are like us and we gravitate towards them. And, sometimes, we do not like people that are unlike us and we shun them. This may be the law of self-preservation at work: we preserve who we are or what we are in other people. A dishonest person that is involved in corruption will avoid an honest one that is clean out of fear of exposure. Likewise an honest, clean person will shun the dishonest, corrupt one out of fear of being label the same. My assumption? Become what you want to attract in others, to a certain extent, and you will begin to recognize the real people from the charlatan ones. Birds of a feather usually flock together.

Who we are attract like-minded people to us. Those who do wrong things and those who do things the wrong way, but neither recognize nor accept that they are wrong, are very dangerous people. Keep them around you at your own peril.

I got the following from one Dr Dayton Campbell MP's Facebook wall: I think it is relevant here. It says: "If numbers in Mathematics were given an opportunity to speak, I think some were going to accuse zero and one. But why accusing zero and 1. Relax. Any number that is multiplied by zero gives zero. Zero will bring down numbers to nothing. There are some people in life who are like number zero. If you associate with them no matter how great your value is they will bring you down to zero. How about one? Any number multiplied by one remains unchanged no matter how big it is. There are some people in life that are like one. No matter how they touch your life you remain the same. You don't grow, you don't improve, and you remain at the same level. So here is the twist. What kind of person are you and who do you associate with? May God separate us from everyone carrying the spirit of Zero (0) and One (1). May HE also help us grow and be greater than 1 so that when we touch the lives of others, we will add value..."

I have heard of some people that believe that money rituals, sowing seeds, or paying tithes will make them rich. I think this is where the saying that "faith without work is dead" is applicable. Mark Zuckerberg simply developed his human capital to the point of excellence. "Human capital is the stock of knowledge, habits, social and personality attributes, including creativity, embodied in the ability to perform labor so as to produce economic value." By focusing on developing and increasing your human capitals, like Mark did, all the other capitals, of which financial is one, will be yours on the long run. "...The only reason the season of mango will yield mango fruits is if a mango tree was already standing ahead of the season..." ~ **Olajide Abiola.**

The development of Mark's human capital unavoidably gave him excellent social capital. Social capital is "the networks of relationships among people who live and work in a particular society, enabling that society to function effectively." Social capital "consists of the economic resources garnered from human interactions. The resources include those of tangible and non-tangible assets, such as information, innovative ideas, and financial support." It is just as valuable as financial capital. The more you develop your human capital, the more social capital you are going to have. And, the more financial capital you are going to have on the long run. The following story showcases the path that Mark went through to become one of the youngest billionaire in the world: Mark Elliot Zuckerberg was born on May 14, 1984, in White Plains, New York, into a comfortable, well-educated family, and raised in the nearby village of Dobbs Ferry. His father, Edward Zuckerberg, ran a dental practice attached to the family's home. His mother, Karen, worked as a psychiatrist. Zuckerberg developed an interest in computers at an early age; when he was about 12, he used Atari BASIC to create a messaging program he named "Zucknet." His father used the program in his dental office, so that the receptionist could inform him of a new patient without yelling across the room. The family also used Zucknet to communicate within the house. Together with his friends, he also created computer games just for fun. "I had a bunch of friends who were artists," he said. "They'd come over, draw stuff, and I'd build a game out of it."

To keep up with Mark's burgeoning interest in computers, his parents hired private computer tutor David Newman to come to the house once a week and work with Mark. Newman later told reporters that it was hard to stay ahead of the prodigy, who began taking graduate courses at nearby Mercy College around this same time.

Zuckerberg remained fascinated by computers, and continued to work on developing new programs. While still in high school, he created an early version of the music software Pandora, which he called Synapse. Several companies—including AOL and Microsoft—expressed an interest in buying the software, and hiring the teenager before graduation. He declined the offers.

Zuckerberg enrolled at Harvard University. By his sophomore year at the Ivy League Institution, he had developed a reputation as the go-to software developer on campus. It was at that time that he built a program called CourseMatch, which helped students choose their classes based on the course selections of other users. He also invented Facemash, which compared the pictures of two students on campus and allowed users to vote on which one was more attractive. The program became wildly popular, but was later shut down by the school administration after it was deemed inappropriate.

Based on the buzz of his previous projects, three of his fellow students—Divya Narendra, and twins Cameron and Tyler Winklevoss—sought him out to work on an idea for a social networking site they called Harvard Connection. This site was designed to use information from Harvard's student networks in order to create a dating site for the Harvard elite. Zuckerberg agreed to help with the project, but soon dropped out to work on his own social networking site with friends Dustin Moskovitz, Chris Hughes and Eduardo Saverin. Zuckerberg and his friends created a site that allowed users to create their own profiles, upload photos, and communicate with other users. The group ran the site—first called The Facebook—out of a dorm room at Harvard until June 2004. After his sophomore year, Zuckerberg dropped out of college to devote himself to Facebook full time, moving the company to Palo Alto, California. By the end of 2004, Facebook had 1 million users. In 2005, Zuckerberg's enterprise received a huge boost from the venture capital firm Accel Partners. Accel invested $12.7 million into the network, which at the time was open only to Ivy League students. Zuckerberg's company then granted access to other colleges, high school and international schools, pushing the site's membership to more than 5.5 million users by December 2005. The site then began attracting the interest of other companies, who wanted to advertize with the popular social hub. Not wanting to sell out, Zuckerberg turned down offers from companies such as Yahoo! and MTV Networks. Instead, he focused on expanding the site, opening up his project to outside developers and adding more features. Source **www.biography.com**

Do you want to create wealth? Get pertinent knowledge and skills. Knowledge and skills are not the same. You can know something, and do not know how to do it. Most of the time, the desired result comes after the doing, not just from mere knowing. You have a burning desire to be successful. But do you have the requisite knowledge and skills? To be successful in anything you do, you have to do more than the infamous "just claim it." Knowledge and skills are something to be acquired, not just hoped for. "Success in life is largely a matter of cultivating effective habits. Habits are combination of desire, knowledge and skills." Water is used for many things. It is used for washing clothes, to make them clean. It is good for drinking, to quench one's thirst at any time. A thirsty, dirty man that brags about having plenty of water, as a matter of fact, the best water there is, may be considered delusional. Where is the effect of water in his life? Ideals are good but practicality is what matters most. "It's the little things that make the big things possible. Only close attention to the fine details of any operation makes the operation first class." ~ **John Willard Marriott.**

As an initial matter, we need to find out what we want tomorrow. Also, we need to find out how to get what we want tomorrow. And, we need to find out what we don't want tomorrow so that we can desist from doing the things that will metamorphose into our tomorrow. Then, we need to begin to do those things in earnest. What works for others may not work for you. Instead of following what works for someone else, something written inside books, one should discover what works for him. It is about self-discovery. Discover yourself. Find out what works for you. Find out what does not. Concentrate your resources of doing what works for you. Refrain from what does not. Prior proper planning has been said to prevent poor performance. And, a well-knitted lifestyle must be planned. Don't leave yours to chance! The reason we put so much effort, so much commitment into any endeavor is to achieve desirable and favorable result, within reasonable time frame. If the effort, the commitment is coupled with the right and truthful knowledge, thinking/beliefs, it will yield the desired, favourable result. But if the effort, the commitment is coupled with half truths, lies, and delusions, the desired, favourable result will never come, leading to frustration, anger, and disappointment. Get rid of delusion, and half-truths, outright lies will disappear, taking frustration, anger and disappointment with them.

"Be always at war with your vices, at peace with your neighbors, and let each new year find you a better man." ~ **Benjamin Franklin**. Shrink your appetites. Distend your scruples. Associate with valuable friends. Select the company you keep with utmost care. Mindsets are contagious. Limit your time with those who fail to develop the millionaire mindset. Cultivate a pleasing personality. Be creative and innovative. Focus on developing and increasing your human capital and all the other capitals, of which financial is, one, will be yours on the long run. The result you get from fake product is the same result you get from fake people: ultimate disappointment. Find real people with correct principles and surround yourself with them. How do you find them? Become one. Develop the habit of keeping your words, in small things and big ones. This is how to develop a strong reputation for reliability and trustworthiness. Be authentic.

Say what you mean and mean what you say. Stick to your values and principles at all times. Let the law of attraction take care of the rest. Just because you want to create wealth does not mean you are going to attract wealth. You must continually develop and hone your human and social capitals. The foundation of tomorrow's success is laid, one block at a time, yesterday and today. To be successful tomorrow requires learning and development today.

CHAPTER 8

CREATING WEALTH

"An investment in knowledge pays the best interest". ~ **Benjamin Franklin.**

Can anyone be rich? Robert Toru Kiyosaki thinks so. The following is what he said about that. "Yes, I believe everyone has the potential to be rich. Our mindsets have the power to make us rich or poor. The leverage of our mind is very important. The words we use can either make us rich or poor.' Robert Toru Kiyosaki is an American businessman and author. Kiyosaki is the founder of the Rich Dad Company, a private financial education company that provides personal finance and business education to people through books and videos. ~**Wikipedia.**

Everyone has the opportunity to acquire wealth, but not everyone seizes the opportunity. You may not be able to get rich by sitting in your comfort zone. Do you know that self-employment is the fastest way to create wealth? Self-employed people are called entrepreneurs. Entrepreneurs are people who set up businesses, taking on financial risks in the hope of profit. A lot of people already have the entrepreneurial mindset."An entrepreneur is a person who is willing and able to convert a new idea or invention into a successful business." He or she helps the economy of a country grow and creates new jobs. You need passion, knowledge and skills to grow a business. You also need patience because it takes time to grow a business. "To be successful, you must decide exactly what you want to accomplish, and then resolve to pay the price to get it.' Entrepreneurs create something new, something different—they change or transmute value.

People that have created wealth are not superhuman. They are regular people like you and me. For example, look at Jeff Bezos: Who Is Jeff Bezos?

Early Life and Career

Jeff Bezos was born on January 12, 1964, in Albuquerque, New Mexico, to a teenage mother, Jacklyn Gise Jorgensen, and his biological father, Ted Jorgensen. The Jorgensens were married less than a year, and when Bezos was 4 years old his mother re-married, to Cuban immigrant Mike Bezos. As a child, Jeff Bezos showed an early interest in how things work, turning his parents' garage into a laboratory and rigging electrical contraptions around his house. He moved to Miami with his family as a teenager, where he developed a love for computers and graduated valedictorian of his high school. It was during high school that he started his first business, the Dream Institute, an educational summer camp for fourth, fifth and sixth graders.

Bezos pursued his interest in computers at Princeton University, where he graduated summa cum laude in 1986 with a degree in computer science and electrical engineering. After graduation, he found work at several firms on Wall Street, including Fitel, Bankers Trust and the investment firm D.E. Shaw. It was there he met his wife, Mackenzie, and became the company's youngest vice president in 1990.

While his career in finance was extremely lucrative, Bezos chose to make a risky move into the nascent world of e-commerce. He quit his job in 1994, moved to Seattle and targeted the untapped potential of the internet market by opening an online bookstore.

Launching Amazon.com

Bezos set up the office for his fledgling company in his garage where, along with a few employees, he began developing software. They expanded operations into a two-bedroom house, equipped with three Sun Microstations, and eventually developed a test site. After inviting 300 friends to beta test the site, Bezos opened Amazon.com, named after the meandering South American River, on July 16, 1995.The initial success of the company was meteoric. With no press promotion, Amazon.com sold books across the United States and in 45 foreign countries within 30 days. In two months, sales reached $20,000 a week, growing faster than Bezos and his start-up team had envisioned.

Amazon.com went public in 1997, leading many market analysts to question whether the company could hold its own when traditional retailers launched their own e-commerce sites. Two years later, the start-up not only kept up, but also outpaced competitors, becoming an e-commerce leader. Bezos continued to diversify Amazon's offerings with the sale of CDs and videos in 1998, and later clothes, electronics, toys and more through major retail partnerships. While many dot.coms of the early '90s went bust, Amazon flourished with yearly sales that jumped from $510,000 in 1995 to over $17 billion in 2011.

In 2006, Amazon.com launched its video on demand service; initially known as Amazon Unbox on TiVo, it was eventually rebranded as AmazonInstant Video. In 2007, the company released the Kindle, a handheld digital book reader that allowed users to buy, download, read and store their book selections. That same year, Bezos announced his investment in Blue Origin, a Seattle-based aerospace company that develops technologies to offer space travel to paying customers. Bezos entered Amazon into the tablet marketplace with the unveiling of the Kindle Fire in 2011. The following September, he announced the new Kindle Fire HD, the company's next generation tablet designed to give Apple's iPad a run for its money. "We haven't built the best tablet at a certain price. We have built the best tablet at any price," Bezos said, according to ABC News.

Buying 'The Washington Post'

Bezos made headlines worldwide on August 5, 2013, when he purchased The Washington Post and other publications affiliated with its parent company, The Washington Post Co., for $250 million. The deal marked the end of the four-generation reign over The Post Co. by the Graham family, which included Donald E. Graham, the company's chairman and chief executive, and his niece, Post publisher Katharine Weymouth. "The Post could have survived under the company's ownership and been profitable for the foreseeable future," Graham stated, in an effort to explain the transaction. "But we wanted to do more than survive. I'm not saying this guarantees success, but it gives us a much greater chance of success." In a statement to Post employees on August 5, 2013 Bezos wrote: "The values of The Post do not need changing... There will, of course, be change at The Post over the coming years. That's essential and would have happened with or without new ownership. The internet is transforming almost every element of the news business: shortening news cycles, eroding long-reliable revenue sources, and enabling new kinds of competition, some of which bear little or no news-gathering costs. There is no map, and charting a path ahead will not be easy. We will need to invent, which means we will need to experiment. Our touchstone will be readers, understanding what they care about—government, local leaders, restaurant openings, scout troops, businesses, charities, governors, sports—and working backwards from there. I'm excited and optimistic about the opportunity for invention."

Amazon Prime & Amazon Studios

In early December 2013, Bezos made headlines when he revealed a new, experimental initiative by Amazon, called "Amazon Prime Air," using drones—remote-controlled machines that can perform an array of human tasks—to provide delivery services to customers. According to Bezos, these drones are able to carry items weighing up to five pounds, and are capable of traveling within a 10-mile distance of the company's distribution center. He also stated that Prime Air could become a reality within as little as four or five years.

Bezos oversaw one of Amazon's few major missteps when the company launched the Fire Phone in 2014; criticized for being too gimmicky, it was discontinued the following year. However, Bezos did score a victory with the development of original content through Amazon Studios. After premiering several new programs in 2013, Amazon hit it big in 2014 with the critically acclaimed Transparent and Mozart in the Jungle. In 2015, the company produced and released Spike Lee's Chi-Raq as its first original feature film. In 2016, Bezos stepped in front of the camera for a cameo appearance playing an alien in Star Trek Beyond. A Star Trek fan since childhood, Bezos is listed as a Starfleet Official in the movie credits on IMDb. In July 2017, Bezos briefly surpassed Microsoft founder Bill Gates to become the richest person in the world, according to Bloomberg, before dropping back to No. 2. The Amazon chief then reclaimed the top spot in October, and in January 2018, Bloomberg pegged his net worth at $105.1 billion, making him the richest person in history. Two months later, Bezos was up to $127 billion, equal to the combined wealth of 2.3 million average Americans, before continuing his surge to the $150 billion plateau in mid-July.

Healthcare Venture

On January 30, 2018, Amazon, Berkshire Hathaway and JPMorgan Chase delivered a joint press release in which they announced plans to pool their resources to form a new healthcare company for their U.S. employees. According to the release, the company will be "free from profit-making incentives and constraints" as it tries to find ways to cut costs and boost satisfaction for patients, with an initial focus on technology solutions. "The healthcare system is complex, and we enter into this challenge open-eyed about the degree of difficulty," said Bezos. "Hard as it might be, reducing healthcare's burden on the economy while improving outcomes for employees and their families would be worth the effort." Not long afterward, The Seattle Times reported that more changes were afoot for Amazon, with the company consolidating its consumer retail operations in order to focus on Alexa, AWS, digital entertainment and other growing areas. An Amazon spokesperson confirmed the news, saying, "As part of our annual planning process, we are making head count adjustments across the company — small reductions in a couple of places and aggressive hiring in many others." In April 2018, as part of his annual shareholder letter, Bezos said the company had surpassed 100 million paid subscribers for AmazonPrime. He added that 2017 had been an outstanding year for hardware sales, and that Amazon would continue to invest in expanding its customer base, brand and infrastructure." Jeff Bezos: Business Leader, Entrepreneur. Biography source: **www.biography.com.**

Let me talk about a pattern I have noticed among some people that want to create wealth. Let us say I write about a doctor who owns and runs his own clinic. This doctor is married with beautiful children. And he is financially and emotionally successful. Many of these people will like the story. Vicariously, they are him. Or they will like to be like him when they get to his age but when I write about the duties, sacrifices, discipline that precede being a doctor, only a few of these people will like the story. They fail to realize the correlation between those two stories. Cause and effect, action and reaction, rights and duties are irrevocably linked. You have to do something, give up something, to get something. Manna may have fallen during antiquity time. But I have not seen any in my lifetime although I have seen corruption as spoils of office, mimicking true blessings.

Start by acquiring a marketable skill. Marketable skill can be acquired from training or life experience. Work hard to harness the skill. Ideas, opportunities, partners, and money will naturally follow. Identify a business opportunity. What are the necessary resources needed? Acquire and deploy the necessary resources required for the exploitation of the identified business opportunity. Shift economic resources out of an area of lower yield into an area of higher productivity and greater yield. Add emotional maturity and integrity to the mixture as you will not continue to patronize a business where you are treated rudely and defrauded. Your money making business will not only thrive, it will triumph. To be more specific, you have to do some things right to get the right things. To get the right output, which is to create wealth, the input and process must be right. Failure to do this will only, on the long run, result in disappointment, frustration, and anger. And consequently, unhappiness, unfulfillment, and stagnation will set in, likely to be passed on to the next generation as its inheritance. So, if someone invites you to come and make money, and it sounds easy, you are not likely to make money but to spend it. Wealth creation requires hard work, diligence and consistency.

Knowledge is what you know. Skill is what you can do well with what you know. Skills bring knowledge to life. You want to start your own business and create wealth? Selling is a skill. And, selling something of value is one way to make money, to create wealth. You can either produce something of value or you can help to distribute something of value produced by others. Another word for selling is commerce. Commerce is defined as the activity of buying and selling, especially on a large scale. And e-commerce is commercial transactions conducted electronically on the Internet.

Do you have the capacity and willingness to develop, organize, and manage a business venture in order to make a profit? Then you are an entrepreneur and you have the millionaire mindset. Every human has the potential to create wealth. But potential is not actual. Yet, potential can be transformed into actual with the mastery of the input-process-output model. In order to do this, we need power. What is power? It is simply the ability to achieve. What can we do without power? Mostly nothing. Therefore understanding power is absolutely necessary. These are the types of power formulated by social psychologists John R. P. French and Bertram Raven in 1959 and 1965.

(1) Legitimate power.

(2) Reward power

(3) Expert power.

(4) Referent power.

(5) Coercive power

(6) Informational power.

(7) Connection power.

Legitimate power is formal power. As an elected leader in any political party, either for the party, state, or national office, you have legitimate power. Legitimate power is also called authority power. Are you participating in the political process in your neighborhood? Are you imbibing the values and mores of your preferred party? Apart from giving you robust social capital, it will also enrich your cultural capital. Cultural capital is the accumulation of knowledge, behaviors, and skills that one can tap into to demonstrate one's cultural competence, and thus one's social status or standing in society. Another example of authority power is: if we see a policeman with a gun, we know that he has the formal power to carry the gun because he represents authority and, therefore, authorized to carry arms.

Reward power is the ability to reward anyone who has done something for us. Financial capital is an example of reward power. Financial capital is the money, credit, and other forms of funding that build wealth. We also use financial capital to invest.

Expert power is when we possess the knowledge and skills to get some things done effectively. It is the same as human capital. "Human capital is the stock of knowledge, habits, social and personality attributes, including creativity, embodied in the ability to perform labor so as to produce economic value."

"**Referent power** is gained by a leader who has strong interpersonal relationship skills. Referent power, as an aspect of personal power, becomes particularly important as organizational leadership is increasingly about collaboration and influence rather than command and control." ~ **Wikipedia**. Referent power requires emotional maturity. Emotional maturity is defined when you have the ability to experience these emotions and then quickly let them go. People who are immature seem to remain stuck in these negative emotions, unable to get past them. Emotional maturity is the ability to see life clearly and accurately, and to deal with it effectively. No matter the emotion that is running through one, it is not advisable to displease those that "hold the horns of the wild cow" unless one is willing and able to "hold the horns of the wild cow" himself/herself.

Coercive power is to be able to force others to do what we want them to do even if they do not want to do it.

Information power is to possess timely, accurate, and pertinent information.

"**Connection power** is where a person attains influence by gaining favor or simply acquaintance with a powerful person. This power is all about networking." Connection power is a component of social capital. **Social capital** is "the networks of relationships among people who live and work in a particular society, enabling that society to function effectively." It "consists of the economic resources garnered from human interactions. The resources include those of tangible and non-tangible assets, such as information, innovative ideas, and financial support." "Social capital is as valuable as financial capital."

Do you want to create wealth? Start with creating value. What services can you render that is valuable to your customers? What products meet your customers' expectations do you have to sell? Do you own any asset that has economic value-creating capacity such as skills and experience in a particular field? Do you have the type of knowledge that can enable your clients to perform better? Are you focused, disciplined, and competent? Creating wealth requires focus, discipline and competence. Identify a need. Set your target audience. Create a solution. Define your vision. Choose a business name. Register the business. Open a business account. Establish online presence. Create a structure. Sell, sell, and sell.

"Faith is a state of mind through which your aims, desires, plans and purposes may be translated into their physical or financial equivalent."

Faith without work is said to be dead. Prayer is an act of faith. It is not work. Beliefs are elements of faith. They are not work. Tithing, seeding, night vigils etc are religious rituals. They are not work. What, then, is this work that is so fundamental to making faith come alive? In modern language, it is the input-process-output model. This is the foundation of all things produced by humans. Those who have mastered, and continually implement the input-process-output model, not only succeed, but also created wealth. Those who ignore it, fail.

What is input-process-output model? Let us say you want to always have food in your house. Becoming a farmer will be one good option. Acquiring lands, farm helps, seedlings etc are quintessential. That is your input. The actual cultivation of the lands, weeding and watering, etc, that is your process. Aha! The harvest, the real reason behind your striving, that is your output.

Our inheritance is our fate. This inheritance includes our genetic makeup, the country we are born in, our early classical conditioning etc. We can use our inheritance as mere input. Or we can use it as our destiny. Those who use inheritance that fate gave them as destiny may find it difficult to change their destiny. But those who use the inheritance that fate gave them as mere input will adopt, invent, learn the processes to turn that input into favorable and desirable output, thereby changing or improving their destiny from the one fate gave them. We are not as powerless as we may have thought.

Factors of production are said to be land, labor, capital, and entrepreneurial ability. These four factors of production are the resources required for generation of goods or services.

1. Land (including all natural resources).
2. Labor (including all human resources).
3. Capital (including all man-made resources).
4. Entrepreneurship (which brings all the previous resources together for production).

These four factors of production are the inputs used in the production process to produce output - that is, finished goods and services.

A business plan is a critical component of a successful business. It is one of the vital documents in the arsenal of anyone with a millionaire mindset. What is a Business Plan? "A business plan is a document that describes a new business, its products or services, how it will earn money, leadership and staffing, financing, operations model, and other details that are essential to both operation and success. Entrepreneurs create them as part of the startup process while existing businesses often write them when changing direction or strategy. Most business plans cover the company's first three to five years." ~ **Business Encyclopedia**. "A business plan is a formal statement of business goals, reasons they are attainable, and plans for reaching them. It may also contain background information about the organization or team attempting to reach those goals. Written business plans are often required to obtain a bank loan or other financing."

"Productivity is never an accident. It is always the result of a commitment to excellence, intelligent planning and focused effort." ~ **Paul J. Meyer**. To achieve excellent productivity, we need the right combination of powers. Without the right combination, we may suffer from "illusion of power", and achievement of objectives/goals may be elusive. And, those without appropriate types of power blame external factors for their woes. They may even believe that their family is cursed. Most of the time, the problem is "within". And our intelligence, with its intuitive component firing, can assist in, not only solving problems, but also in preempting and preventing problems. Intelligence is not just the ability to learn and understand. It is also the ability to cope with new and trying situations. The usage of intelligence can be an antidote to the prevention and resolution of most problems. The best time to lay the foundation of today's success, one block at a time, was yesterday. The best time to lay the foundation of tomorrow's success, one block at a time, is today.

Creativity is one of the easiest ways to create wealth in one generation. Creativity is the easiest for those that are creative, for those that have mastered the creative process. One creative product may be worth millions. Do you think of yourself as a creative personality? "If you do, you are both fortunate and correct, in fact the beautiful truth is that everyone is creative and we all have the ability to develop our creative potential. It is wise to remember that the person who follows the crowd will get no further than the crowd. The person who walks the creative path is likely to find they are in places no one has ever been before." ~ **Bob Proctor**. What is Creativity? "Creativity is the ability to replace old, familiar patterns of living and problem- solving with new and equally, or more successful ones. Not only is creativity the ability to find solutions for life's problems in the world around us, it is also the ability to rearrange intrapsychic patterns that threaten to block self-expression without which there can be no creativity."

"Creativity goes hand in hand with innovation. And there is no innovation without creativity. While creativity is the ability to produce new and unique ideas, innovation is the implementation of that creativity - that's the introduction of a new idea, solution, process, or product. Creativity is the driving force behind innovation and the incorporation of looking at things from a different perspective and freedom of restrictions by rules and written or unwritten norms."

Innovation is "The process of translating an idea or invention into a good or service that creates value or for which customers will pay. To be called an innovation, an idea must be replicable at an economical cost and must satisfy a specific need. Innovation involves deliberate application of information, imagination and initiative in deriving greater or different values from resources, and includes all processes by which new ideas are generated and converted into useful products. In business, innovation often results when ideas are applied by the company in order to further satisfy the needs and expectations of the customers." Some people may be primed to be more creative than others, but nearly everyone is said to be born with some level of creative ability. Therefore, anyone can develop the skills to be creative or not to be creative "Creative thinking requires using the resources of the mind to come up with ideas that have not been thought of before. It requires knowledge, logic, imagination and intuition. To be considered creative, idea must not only be new, but must also be valued. Valued ideas are those that improve products, processes or sense of well-being. To think creatively, one must, as a basic rule, want to have novel thought. Those who are firmly tied to prevailing thoughts may reject novel thoughts even if the thoughts jump into their minds." It is true that knowledge is basic to good creative thinking. But it is not enough. Knowledge must be digested so that it emerges in the form of fresh, new ideas and insights. That is a function of intuition. Some environments are more conducive for the blooming of creativity than others. Creativity flourishes more in societies that cherish divergent thinking. It is easily stifled in societies where convergent thinking is more valuable.

"If you want to change your life, first you must change your thoughts." Mindset is mostly everything. "The mind is the limit; as long as the mind can envision the fact that you can do something, you can do it, as long as you really believe 100 percent" ~ Arnold Schwarzenegger. More gold is said to have been mined from the thoughts of man than has been taken from the earth. "Thinking is powerful. Knowing is even more so. Thinking is a function of your mind. Knowing encompasses all you are. What you think can change from moment to moment. What you know is always a part of you. What you know goes beyond all doubt. What you know has the clear, powerful presence of truth. Use your outstanding mind to think. Use your magnificent life to know. Knowing comes from experience, guided by purpose, and from feeling the wonder of all existence. Know that you can do it, that you can be it, that you can experience it, and you will." ~ **Ralph Marston.**

To innovate is essentially to change something and make it better. Have you been thinking new thoughts lately? Or are you simply rehashing old thoughts? You want to do better than the way you are doing right now? You have to think different. If we cannot rearrange our thinking, we cannot innovate. And, if we cannot innovate, we will stagnate. If we cannot produce new thoughts, we cannot produce something that is original, that is worthwhile. If we cannot produce something that is original, that is worthwhile, we cannot produce favorable and desirables products and services. If we cannot produce favorable goods and services, our country's currency will continue to lose value. "Gold mines tap out. Stock markets crash. Real estate investments can go sour. But a human mind with the ability to think well is like a diamond mine that never runs out. It's priceless."

If we have been doing it before, let us find another way to do it better. That is innovation. If we, or anyone else, have not done it before, let us find a way to start doing it. Let us replace the old, familiar one with a new, better one. That is creativity. Let us keep doing it because that is the way it has always been done. That is conservatism, and stagnation on the long run. All progressive businesses embrace creativity and innovation. And all regressing, stagnating businesses disdain creativity and innovation. It is time to embrace creativity and innovation. Doing the same things the way we have always done them will only result in getting the same things we have always gotten.

Always remember that anything left by themselves will go from bad to worse if nothing is done to prevent that.

CHAPTER 9

THE MILLIONAIRE MINDSET IN POLITICS

"One of the penalties for refusing to participate in politics is that you end up being governed by your inferiors". - **Plato** ~ **BrainyQuote.**

A lot of people sit in their comfortable homes, unwilling to participate in grassroots politics. But politics is about power. And power has been defined as the ability to achieve. Without power, good governance will remain a midget, at the mercy of impunity and corruption. The millionaire mindset is very compatible with the acquisition and skillful usage of legitimate power/authority power.

Political parties are "power houses" where all members deposit their power to make the party supreme. And there are those within the party that have been elected, or selected, and consequently have been conferred with leadership and authority power. It is therefore clear that the authority power of the party leadership is lethal to anyone at loggerhead with the leadership of his or her party. He or she will "bleed", not blood, but power even if he or she is committed to good governance. Anyone not in sync with the party's values and norms will not be rewarded with bigger power to govern.

My sympathy is always with those that "hold the horns of the wild cow", not with those "milking" it. Building any structure, whether in business, politics, or any other area of human achievement is a tough and tedious job. Those who have done so successfully are the ones I likened to "holding the horns of a wild cow." Those party people, both the generals and the foot soldiers, are the ones on the battlefield in our quest to get good governance. Their values and quality will definitely be reflected in the type of governance we get. No matter the emotion that is running through one, it is not advisable to displease those that "hold the horns of the wild cow" unless one is willing and able to "hold the horns of the wild cow" himself/herself. If the existing structure does not fit your personality and conscience, build your own. This may be a wakeup call for those that want good governance but abhor "dirty" politics.

As an elected, selected, or otherwise leader in any political party, either for the party, state, or national office, you also have legitimate power. Like I said earlier, legitimate power is also called authority power.

Legitimate power/authority power is formal power. Yes, an elected legislator, governor or president has legitimate power derived from the Constitution. But in Nigeria, the same constitution does not make any provision for independent candidate. The implication of this is, for anyone to be elected in the first place, he or she must belong to a political party. Political parties are therefore, foundational to the acquisition of political power.

I advise you to continue to develop your human capital. Are you interested in qualitative, principled governance? Are you participating in the political process in your neighborhood? Are you imbibing the values and mores of your preferred party? Apart from giving you robust social capital, which is as valuable as financial capital, it will also enrich your cultural capital. Cultural capital is the accumulation of knowledge, behaviors, and skills that one can tap into to demonstrate one's cultural competence, and thus one's social status or standing in society. Cultural capital has great electoral value.

A highly developed human capital will always be in demand. Anyone that has not developed his or her human capital up to an acceptable level may find it difficult to rise through the file and rank of his or her preferred political party. Yes, loyalty is a component of human capital. Intelligence and creativity are also part of human capital. Any organization that wants to grow will always develop its human resources. If particular knowledge/skills cannot be found within the organization, the organization will seek for it from outside the organization. This is prudent strategic management and nothing else.

Apart from the popular culture, there is also something called organizational culture. Organizational culture is the underlying beliefs, assumptions, values and ways of interacting that contribute to the unique social and psychological environment of an organization. Organizational culture includes an organization's expectations, experiences, philosophy, as well as the values that guide member behavior, and is expressed in member self-image, inner workings, interactions with the outside world, and future expectations. Culture is based on shared attitudes, beliefs, customs, and written and unwritten rules that have been developed over time and are considered valid (**The Business Dictionary**). Culture also includes the organization's vision, values, norms, systems, symbols, language, assumptions, beliefs, and habits (**Needle, 2004**). I knew this much. That was why I wrote the following few years ago: if I join politics, I will eventually be expelled for anti party activities. My pen is famously loyal to my conscience. And my conscience is loyal to truths only. Blind loyalty to the political party, even when the party is clearly wrong, is not compatible with my soul. It is important to recognize that anyone that wants to enjoy certain rights within any organization cannot be freed from all the obligations connected with those rights. If you are going to be a political party man, be a good one.

The same millionaire mindset that is required to excel as an honest party man or business man is the same to excel as a corrupt person. The only difference is that one uses the virtues of consistency and persistency for what is right and the other for what is bad. Maurice Ibekwe was probably a good party man. Maurice Ibekwe was a PDP member of the House of Representatives from Imo State. He was elected in 1999. He was the Chairman, House Committee on Police and Internal Security.

In 2003, Maurice Ibekwe, who represented Okigwe North Federal Constituency at the lower house, was accused of advanced fee fraud, "419." Operatives of the EFCC swung into action and arrested him and a few others. They were brought to a Lagos High Court on the allegation of obtaining money under false pretense, an offense frowned at by Section 419 of the Nigerian Criminal Code, hence the acronym 419 for advance fee fraud. Advance-fee fraud is a form of fraud that appears to be a field in which Nigerian entrepreneurs were pioneers, and remain prominent. The scammers are frequently viewed as a sort of folk hero or Robin Hood, getting money out of gullible westerners in repayment for colonial mistreatment. ~ **Wikipedia.**

Ideally, the offense for which he was charged was bailable. But the EFCC convinced the courts to deny him that privilege. His lawyers took the bail denial to the Appeal Court and it was also denied. He became ill during his trial. He came to trial sick, on his wheelchair. He presented medical documents to show that he needed to attend to his ill health. But the judges refused to consider it, insisting that bail is at the discretion of the judge. Maurice Ibekwe was remanded in detention until he died miserably in 2004.

Seeking to create wealth illegally exposes our lives to great danger. It may set one backwards for many years. I know this for a fact.

Ishola Oyenusi popularly known as Dr. Ishola was a Nigerian armed robber who was active during the 1970s. His modus operandi was carjacking, bank robberies and heists committed during hold-ups. ~ **Wikipedia.**

Rumor had it that he stole and sold a car for ₦400 at the time so that he could give his broke girlfriend money she needed. The terrible spin to this story was that he killed the owner of the car during the robbery. "During the time when he was in his prime, he was actually the king of Nigerian gangsters. He was probably the first serious armed robber in Nigeria. His daringness became legendary. He was so insanely brave that he dared to declare that bullets had no power against him. The entire nation was doing its best to catch him but he managed to escape. Finally, in 1971, he was caught after a robbery, in which he got $28,000. A police officer was murdered during the robbery. In accordance with the information received from one of the lawyers who saw him in prison, Oyenusi was first jailed at the age of 21. Then, he escaped and was jailed again. This repeated eight times and then decided to become an armed robber. There's an opinion that the main cause of his rage and cruelty was his poverty. Some witnesses claim that several minutes before his death, Oyenusi told the reporters that he would have never become a criminal if only his parents had enough money to let him go to school. Admitting this, he has also confessed to participating in 10 big robberies with murders within the recent six years." Source: **Evelyn Bankole www.naija.com.**

Oyenusi together with six other members of his gang were executed on 8 September 1971 by a combined police and armed forces firing brigade. He was smiling as the bullets sent him to his grave. His execution was caught on film.

"On the day when Doctor Oyenusi was to be executed, more than 30,000 Nigerians gathered around the execution venue. They gathered in order to show the daring terrorist how helpless he was now and how much they wanted revenge for all the long months of living in terror. Many within the crowd were whistling and mocking the bandit but his friends and relatives did not hide their tears. Oyenusi was smiling up to the end but everybody saw that he was surviving an agony. Several moments before the execution, he finally admitted that he was dying for all the crimes he had committed. The execution was conducted by police and military officers. Reporters filmed the process for all those who were at home beside their TV sets, waiting to see the death of the most horrible robber in modern Nigeria. Oyenusi could not end his life alone. He had six of his gang members executed by his side. They all participated in the last robbery of a Lagos factory. The gang members who always accompanied Oyenusi were executed on the Victoria Island. However, even after their execution, several years later, when there appeared an idea to make a movie about Doctor Oyenusi, actors were afraid to play because they feared the rage of members of the dreadful gang who were probably still alive at that time." Source: **Evelyn Bankole www.naija.com.**

CHAPTER 10

NATURE VERSUS NURTURE

The ability to think straight, some knowledge of the past, some vision of the future, some skills to do useful service, some urges to fit that service into the well-being of the community... These are the most vital things education must try to produce." ~ **Virginia Gildersleave, Dean Emeritus, Barnard College.**

What is that thing that prevents people that are living undesirable and unfavorable life from changing it? Do they not realize that they cannot change their undesirable and unfavorable conditions without changing the fundamental thinking/beliefs that underpin their lives? Are they not familiar with cause and consequences, sowing and reaping? Are they not cognizant that the seeds for their conditions may have been planted in the generations before them? I see a lot of people with innate intelligence but with warped thinking born out of generational ignorance living unfulfilled and unsatisfactory lives. This ought not to be.

People with refined thinking solve problems easily and consequently do not experience too many self-created challenges. Their refined thinking is cognizant of causes, consequences, and cures. They are aware that "assets" acquired yesterday could turned to "liabilities" today.

Error in thinking or false beliefs always leads to disappointment and frustration. The antidote for this is realistic thinking. One must be able to see things the way they are, without distortion, and the way things can be. Only then can one begin to act realistically towards the achievement of objectives and goals. As an initial matter, one must have clarity of mind.

Life does not do as it likes, meaning it is not capricious. Behind the apparent worldly chaos, there is order. There are natural laws that govern the universe. That knowledge is accessible to those who strive to access it. Life is art and science combined. The science part is the fixed laws. The art part is what you do, creatively or otherwise, with the fixed part. Nature has provided. But we must nurture. Nature is unkind to those who fail to nurture. Failure to nurture always leads to underdevelopment, to stagnation, then, to retrogression. Failure to nurture up to the point of excellence nearly ruined my life. My initial training in my youthful years was in flying airplane. I obtained my commercial pilot license, with instrument rating, and multi-engine (Land) in 1982. I learnt how to write short stories and articles in 1995. I took a correspondence diploma course in Short Story Writing and Journalism. That is considered acquisition of knowledge and skills, the development of human capital that I have been writing about. I later went on to acquire Bsc Business Administration and MBA in the early 2000s. This is only half story. The detour I took between the first training and the second one was what nearly ruined my life. When I admonish you to do the right things the right way, trust me, I have the battle scars to back up my assertion.

"The happiness of your life depends upon the quality of your thoughts: therefore, guard accordingly, and take care that you

entertain no notions unsuitable to virtue and reasonable nature."
~ **Marcus Aurelius.**

Thinking is the essence of everything created by humans. Thinking can be classified as useful or useless, valuable or valueless, creative or destructive, old or new, ethical or unethical. Thinking that is new and useful, that is creative and valuable, and that is ethical and legal ultimately creates new values for the individual, for the society.

Self-discipline begins with the mastery of cognition. If you do not control your thoughts, you cannot control your needs. Self-discipline calls for a balancing of the emotions of your heart with the reasoning faculty of your head. First of all, let us understand what cognition is. Cognition is "the mental action or process of acquiring knowledge and understanding through thought, experience, and the senses." Capacity is defined as "the maximum amount that something can contain, and the amount that something can produce." To develop is to "grow or cause to grow and become more mature, advanced, or elaborate."

Personal cognitive capacity development is a long-term continual process of acquiring and strengthening mental skills, competencies and abilities of individuals to overcome generational problems in an attempt to gain mastery of happiness and success. It is an approach to individual behavioral change by focusing on understanding the obstacles that inhibit individuals from realizing their cognitive development goals while enhancing the abilities that will allow them to achieve measurable and sustainable results. It is "the process by which individual develop and strengthen their capability over time to achieve social and economic goals, through improvement of knowledge, skills, within a wider social and cultural enabling environment."

"The capacity to learn is a gift; The ability to learn is a skill; The willingness to learn is a choice." ~ **Brian Herbert, House Harkonnen.**

Let us say I tell you that certain door is locked. And, because you believe me, you do not attempt to open that door. That door will remain locked in your mind. And you will never know if that door is open or not, because you, and your mind, have believed that the door is locked. And, for all practical purposes, it will no longer make sense to you to use that door as an exit. Meanwhile, the door is not locked in concrete reality. I have simply misinformed you. But your belief has locked that door in your subjective reality.

It is clear from the above that your belief that the door is locked is a false belief. It is not true because it has misinformation as its foundation. However, a modern invention called the "scientific method" mandates that we verify all things. And a verse in the bible also advises that one should "test all things". It is imperative that any mind that wants to call itself modern must "install" the scientific method into his/her mind. If not, delusion, which is simply false belief, will infiltrate that mind and makes it susceptible to superstition. I have met people that are naturally intelligent, yet whose beliefs limit their thoughts. And consequently, they could not grow intellectually, mentally, beyond those beliefs. Did I just describe one of the recipes of stagnation? Stagnation is the name of the disease that stops one from changing what is not working. The cure? Creativity. This is simply the ability to replace old, familiar pattern of living with a new, better one. Innovation. "Innovation is defined simply as a "new idea, device, or method." "Innovation distinguishes a leader from a follower"... ~ **Steve Jobs.**

"Talent is something which we have in our blood and skill is something which is acquired after hours and hours of constant practice. Remember, a person with skill is always successful because he had already travelled the road which was impossible for him and he made it one day by believing in himself and its efforts. Try Try, until you succeed. Don't quit. Its just mile away to reach the destination."

Every positive change in your life begins with a clear, unequivocal decision that you are going to either do something or stop doing something. ~ **Brian Tracy.**

Some people may make money from what they know. And, still, some make money from who they know. But most people make money from what they do. Do not just do what you do shabbily. Do it knowledgeably. Do it excellently. Push mediocrity away from you. This is how to bid poverty goodbye forever. You should not only meet your customers'/employer's expectation, but you should also exceed it. That is how success is made in those lands not bubbling with corruption, with incompetence.

Learn not to separate ideas from finance. No matter how brilliant an idea is, if there is no money, or other ability to achieve--power---, that idea will just be mere words on a piece of paper. Trying to activate an idea without the required ability to achieve will ultimately lead to frustration, possibly anger, definitely disappointment. Ideals are good. But to me, practicality is what matters most.

Can we achieve anything we want to achieve in life with enough practice? We should be cognizant that our genes set a bound around what we can possibly achieve. However, they do not entirely determine the ultimate outcome. We have a remarkable capacity to improve our performance in nearly any area of life if we train in the correct way. All we need is sustained effort and concentration. Remain focused. Do not overlook small errors. Do not miss daily opportunities for improvement. Be committed to being a lifelong learner. Always explore, experiment, and refine. Some people may be born geniuses, but majority of us are going to get there through effort.

A source of greatness is excellence. Excellence is a vital factor in creating wealth. And excellence can be reached through the continuous refinement of innate talents, innate abilities, of which everyone possesses in one form or another. "Excellence is a talent or quality which is unusually good and so surpasses ordinary standards. It is also used as a standard of performance as measured e.g. through economic indicators. Excellence is a continuously moving target that can be pursued through actions of integrity, being frontrunner in terms of products / services provided that are reliable and safe for the intended users, meeting all obligations and continuously learning and improving in all spheres to pursue the moving target." ~ **Wikipedia.** "Studies have shown that the most important way to achieve excellent performance in fields such as sport, music, professions and scholarships is to practice. Achievement of excellence in such fields commonly requires approximately 10 years of dedication, comprising about 10,000 hours of effort." ~ **Wikipedia.**

Have you done anything, or are you doing something that others can classify as excellent? If not, it is time to join the league of the few that can produce it. Jumping off the mediocre train onto the excellence one is a task that must be done if we must catch up with the rest of the 21st century world. We must transcend. That means we must go over the ordinary limit. "However difficult life may seem, there is ALWAYS something you can do and succeed at." ~ **Stephen Hawking**. Find what it is and give it your best shot. Therefore, go ahead; discover yourself, by yourself, for yourself. Go from ordinary to extraordinary. You have it in you. Maybe? I know I have it in me. As an initial matter, we must begin from within. Thinking, production of thoughts, which ought to be primary, is the essence of all things produced by humans. The world is constantly changing. Stay up to date on new systems, technology, and your industry trends. Have goals. Stay on track with your goals. Break down your larger goals into smaller specific, measurable, achievable, realistic and time-bound objectives. This increases the chances of your success.

Anything that you do, that does not lead or contribute to neither your success nor happiness, or that does not give you competitive advantage in the larger world, scrap it without sentiment. Certain things do become obsolete in life. And stagnation is very real. If you think it is not, just look in some people's lives. What do you see? Growth? Progress? Or stagnation? With the totality of your thinking/beliefs in consideration, are they stagnant, growing, or regressing? This is a question we all ought to ask ourselves.

Growth and stability ought to be constant in our lives. Using outdated thoughts/beliefs is not compatible with growth and not compatible with stability. Just ask your phone of ten years ago. By the way, the scientific method, a modern method of inquiry, starts with an observation, experience, thoughts. Then, hypothesis is formulated. And, facts are gathered to prove or disprove the hypothesis. If the facts prove the veracity of the hypothesis, it is called truth. But if the facts disprove the hypothesis, then, the hypothesis is declared untrue. Therefore, making unverified statement to contradict a known fact is the hallmark of a lazy, shabby thinker, definitely not compatible with growth, progress, stability.

CHAPTER 11

HEALTH IS WEALTH

"So many people spend their health gaining wealth and then have to spend their wealth to regain their health" ~ **A.J. Reb.**

We are often reminded each time we are feeling indisposed or sick that all the monetary wealth in the world is of limited use if we do not have good health, both physically and mentally. "An unhealthy mind, even in a healthy body, will ultimately destroy health." ~ **Manly P. Hall.**

Knowing how to make money is important. However, without a healthy lifestyle, energy levels, mental sharpness, and communication skills can all drop to unproductive levels. In year 2000, I began to get tired easily. And I was weak most of the time. Naturally, I went to see the doctor. Blood work was done. And it revealed that my red blood cells were thin. Anemia was diagnosed. Iron pills were prescribed. Problem seemed to have been solved. But it was not. The more iron pills I swallowed, the more tired, weaker I got. So I went back to the doctor. He was perplexed. But he ordered more blood work. The same result came back. He scratched his head. He was puzzled. Then, a light must have flashed in his head. He recommended that I should go and see a psychologist. What was the business of a psychologist with physical weakness, I thought to myself. But I guessed he made the recommendation based on my medical history.

I did talk with the psychologist. He found nothing wrong with me. And he sent me back to the doctor. I was beginning to get worried. I remembered those Nigerian stories of illness with no cause and cure because they were tagged "spiritual attacks" or the handiwork of witches and wizards. My father was a product of this environment, a typical traditional Nigerian. He believed in witches and wizards. He believed his enemies-which I refused to inherit-were always behind his ailments, his misfortunes. He believed one of my mother's relatives was a witch and that she killed my mother. When I tried to tell him that my friend, a medical doctor, tested and confirmed that my mother died of breast cancer, he said, "won ta lofa ni." "She was shot with spiritual arrow." My youngest brother that died of asthma was killed by my father's enemy, he insisted. Before he died in 2012, at a ripe age of 85, he was still adamant that his ailments were the handiwork of his enemies. "But baba mi, why do all these enemies do all these to you and then leave me untouched, knowing that I was your first born, the person you lean on for assistance?" I asked. My father replied that the enemies' machinations did not work on me because I did not believe. Ah! Seemed like we had a solution. "Baba mi, if what you are saying is true, then stop believing so this thing will not work on you too." Instead of seeing the logical conclusion to his utterance, he simply said that I did not understand. Imagine that. He finally died, not from the machinations of witches, wizards, and enemies, but from prostate cancer, from old age. Just as I did not inherit his enemies, I also did not inherit his believe in witches and wizards. As a modern man who has a modern mind, I know that I can use my thinking, my behavior, to guide the course of my life. Six years after my father's "enemies" killed him, I am still alive, loving, laughing, and enjoying the simple pleasures of life. It is either witches or wizards are figments of my dad's imagination. Or I have used my modern mystical thinking to conquer them. So, who was it that did not understand?

Anyway, fortunately for me, the doctor in my own case had not been culturally conditioned to entertain stories of spiritual attacks, stories of witches and wizards wrecking havoc on the good health of human beings. He gave me another appointment to come back if my condition did not improve. I guessed he needed some more time to ponder, to research, to find out what could be the cause of my tiredness, my weakness.

My condition did not improve. I was sleeping for more than 12 hours a day. The good thing was: the sleep was very pleasurable. I indeed love to sleep. It was, and still is truly one of the simple pleasures of life that I truly enjoy. On the day the doctor schedule for me to come back, I went to his office. He told me he could not find out what was wrong with me. But he booked an appointment for me to see a dietician. He was not leaving any stone untouched. I saw the dietician. She asked me what type of food did I normally eat and how many time did I eat per day. While I was telling her, she was shaking her head in an attempt to tell me that I was doing it all wrong. When she finally spoke, she strongly recommended that I should always eat breakfast that was rich in fiber, instead of skipping breakfast like I had been doing. She advised that I should cut down on the consumption of carbohydrates. My diet of rice, eba, fufu, and pounded yam were mostly carbohydrates. She said that I should eat small portion of food at a time, even if I had to eat five to six times a day. And, finally, she helped me to develop a balanced meal menu.

Consequently, within one week of adhering to the dietician' advice, my vigorous strength returned, the tiredness, weakness disappeared. I was able to go back on the tracks to continue my enjoyable daily walking exercise. And, within a short period of time, I was able to start jogging. The saying 'you are what you eat' is actually quite true. A chain is indeed as strong as its weakest link. Imagine a simple diet change correcting what we thought was a medical issue. This incident happened in 1999, nineteen years ago. And, I have been enjoying good health since then.

The above anecdote is the reason why I recommend the following: Eat Balanced Diet And Exercise Regularly. Eat right. Exercise. Rest well. Socialize and connect with positive, progressive people. Read. Learn continuously. Write. Teach. Listen to good music. Explore nature. Meditate. Treat others with fairness. Success and happiness guaranteed.

Always remember that money is just one aspect of wealth. There is more to wealth than money. Sound health is very necessary for generating wealth. That is why it is said that Health is wealth. Good health ought be one of the most important priorities in life. Do not play with it. To be healthy is to be fit physically and mentally. To be healthy is to be free from disease or ailment. According to World Health Organization (WHO), health is physical, mental and social well-being and not only the absence of disease. A healthy body is required in generating greater revenue and enjoying personal time with friends and family without good health, can you appreciate the sweetness of ice-cold water on a sunny afternoon? I doubt it. Without good health, can you work productively to make tons of money? To generate income, you have to work and that cannot be done if you are sick and incompetent to do physical activities.

Some people are developing Vitamin D deficiencies. This is said to result in an increased risk of such things as cardiovascular disease, cancer, severe asthma in children, and cognitive impairment in the elderly. Because sunlight is our main source of Vitamin D, being outdoors is absolutely important to improve physical and emotional health. Experts believe that we need about 10,000 IU of Vitamin D daily for improved health. And, just 10-20 minutes a day of having exposure to the sun in mid-day will provide 10,000 IU.

CHAPTER 12

CONTENTMENT AS A REWARD

A reward that comes along with the development of a millionaire mindset is contentment. To be content with whatever one has, to continue to grow without greed, to be prudent in financial matters, is to live a simple lifestyle of no stress, no worries. If you claim that you have knowledge, in this case, the knowledge of how to develop the millionaire mindset, and you cannot use that knowledge to live a good quality life that is brimming with satisfaction and contentment, then, that knowledge, in my opinion, is grossly inadequate. He who knows better ought to do better. Even without the real millions in financial capital manifesting yet, your millionaire mindset will allow you to keep living with inner confidence, the conviction that the millions will eventually come because you have done all the right things the right way. The bottom-line is, you will always have enough to feel wealthy. You will no longer worry about money. You have enough saved to do whatever you please because you've cut your coat according to your fabrics. And you no longer spend money on things that are unnecessary.

The following story of the fisherman is an example of contentment as a reward of developing the millionaire mindset. Even if the millions have not manifested yet, one is able to have the inner confidence, lack of stress and worries that having money brings.

"Once a fisherman was sitting near seashore, under the shadow of a tree smoking his beedi. Beedi is a thin, Indian cigarette filled with tobacco flake and wrapped in a tendu or possibly even Piliostigma racemosum leaf tied with a string at one end. Suddenly a rich businessman passing by approached him and enquired as to why he was sitting under a tree smoking and not working. To this the poor fisherman replied that he had caught enough fishes for the day. Hearing this, the rich man got angry and said: why don't you catch more fishes instead of sitting in shadow wasting your time? Fisherman asked: what would I do by catching more fishes? Businessman: you could catch more fishes, sell them and earn more money, and buy a bigger boat. Fisherman: what would I do then? Businessman: you could go fishing in deep waters and catch even more fishes and earn even more money. Fisherman: what would I do then? Businessman: you could buy many boats and employ many people to work for you and earn even more money. Fisherman: what would I do then? Businessman: you could become a rich businessman like me. Fisherman: what would I do then? Businessman: you could then enjoy your life peacefully. Fisherman: isn't that what I am doing now? Moral – You don't need to wait for tomorrow to be happy and enjoy your life. You don't even need to be much richer, more powerful to enjoy life. LIFE is at this moment, enjoy it fully."

As some great men have said "My riches consist not in extent of my possessions but in the fewness of my wants." ~ **Author Unknown Riches**. In my opinion, it's not just about how much money you have, or do not have. It is also a state of mind brimming with contentment, with satisfaction, with fulfillment.

You just have to be able to determine when you have enough to live a good life. Effective management of money is one of the quintessential of living a satisfying and fulfilling life. Expenses must be less than income. If that is not so, bankruptcy is in the offing. Contraction of appetites, not continuous consumption, is a key factor in money management. If 20% of your spending leads to 80% of your satisfaction, you are okay. You, and contentment, are the best of friends. But if 80% of your spending leads to 20% of your satisfaction, you are in trouble. Contentment will be far away from you. And greed will be your constant companion. If you find yourself begging others to sustain your lifestyle, you are in trouble. That's a sign that your income is less than your expenses. Cutting one's coat according to one's fabrics, and not necessarily according to one's size, is an essential factor in living a satisfying, fulfilling life. This is what life experience has taught me. And it works for me. The day it dawned on me that I did not need as much as I thought I needed to be happy, to be satisfied, that was the day that most things became well with me. With, or without a lot of things, I now feel complete, happy, satisfied. If those things come my way, fine. If they do not, fine. My equanimity will not be disturbed by my lack of certain things.

True contentment is not devoid of ambition. It is a state of psychological satisfaction with one's present condition while striving for the realization of other goals. Life is good, not because I have all that I want, but because I am content with what I have. That means I always cut my coat according to my fabrics. I now live in a self-created cocoon. In my cocoon, there is joy. There is love. And there is peace. There is no undue financial burden in my cocoon. I have mastered the art of living within the confine of my meagre means. Anyone bringing strife and discord and problems is not welcome in my cocoon. Anyone bringing undue financial burden born out of penchant for extraneous appetites is definitely not welcome. In my cocoon, there is always light. And there is this marvelous contentment born out of jettisoning of extraneous appetites. In my cocoon, I get the same feeling you get from jetting out of Lagos after dinner, having breakfast and shopping in Dubai, then proceeding to America to party with family and friends. Simply put, I have mastered the art of enjoying the simplest pleasures that life has to offer, I have heard some people calling this luck. But it is not. This is the result of many years of prudent planning, of rearrangement of thoughts and priorities, of washing my hands clean of all illegality and corruption. Now, I live in my cocoon, with clean hands, without rancor, without malice, laughing, loving, and living. There is nothing beyond satisfaction but greed. If you always need more to be satisfied when less can also be satisfying, check your greed level. It may be high.

I do not envy anyone. I never had, and hopefully, never will envy anyone. Some things that others have, I may not have. And that is okay. That is life. We all cannot have the same things. But some things I do have, others do not have also. Again, that is okay. That is life. We all cannot have the same things. I have love, plenty of it. I am always bubbling with inner peace, inner joy. I live. I laugh. And I am content with the things I have. I sow. I reap. I strictly adhere to the immutable law of cause and effect. And I do not covet my neighbors' things. So, I advise you to live, love, laugh, and enjoy the simple pleasures that life has to offer. Life is good, but you must plan it well. A well-knitted lifestyle must be planned and not just hoped for. Proper planning is known to prevent poor performance.

Money is a manifestation of power. But money is not the only manifestation of power. And power is defined as the "ability to achieve". Therefore, you need some sort of power, not just money, to be noticed in any society. After all, Prof. Chinua Achebe and Prof. Wole Soyinka were not noticed by the world because of their money but because of their mental acumen that manifested as literary prowess. Apart from chasing illegal money, chase something that will benefit your society, humanity. Treat money as an important tool, but not the only one. Focus on recognizing and nurturing other types of wealth; self (human capital), relationships (social capital) and values (cultural capital).

We tend to associate wealth with financial abundance. Yes, this is one obvious measure of the term. However, wealth, in my opinion, is not just about how much money you have, or do not have. It is also a state of mind brimming with contentment, with satisfaction, with fulfillment. Wealth is a peaceful and joyous state of mind, not just a bank balance. The freedom to wake up in the morning without an alarm clock, to do as one pleases with one's time, is also a measure of wealth. Money is less valuable if you do not have the time to enjoy it. Also, time is less valuable if you do not have money to spend. Having money and free time to enjoy it is the true financial freedom.

As already written in chapter 3, the fewer things we want, the easier we can get them. And the happier we will be. The more we are content with what we have, the more satisfaction and happiness we will get. By simply contracting my appetite, and distending my scruples, I am now the happiest and the most contented man. I have wrestled with, and conquered all the witches and wizards from my village. They no longer wreck havoc on my personal finance.

I have always maintained that witches and wizards are figment of our imagination, inherited from the primitive era. Now, please tell me quick: Who is the toughest? Witches and wizards exist in someone's world and reside in his head. Consequently, they followed him from his village to the city and wrecked havoc on his personal finance, success and happiness. What a pitiable fellow. Frustration and anger are his gifts from within.

However, witches and wizards do not exist in my world and do not reside in my head. Consequently, they did not follow me from Lagos to New York. I was the one that tampered with my own success by my negative actions. I was the one that frittered my money away by not cultivating effective spending habits. I have since corrected my ways and consistently striving to do the right things the right way. What a bubbling fellow I have become. Recession cannot even touch me. Inner peace and joy are my gifts from within. Now, tell me, who is the toughest?

It is not what is done to us that hurt us most of the time. It is usually our response to what is done to us that hurt us. When I learnt that over twenty three years ago, I decided to put it into practice. Now, I have mastered happiness. No matter what is going on around me, no matter what I have or do not have, I always remain joyous, mostly peaceful, definitely content. As a matter of fact, I have neither been sad, nor discontent in the last eighteen years. The universe continues to conspire in making sure that good things mostly come to me because I have developed the millionaire mindset. That is why my stomach is always sweet. I have already reached the peak of satisfaction and fulfillment. Anything after satisfaction is, in my opinion, nothing but greed. I no longer feed my greed. I am indeed grateful. "Those with a grateful mindset tend to see the message in the mess. And even though life may knock them down, the grateful find reasons, if even small ones, to get up." ~ **Steve Marabol.**

CONCLUSION

"If you know how to spend less than you get, you have the philosopher's stone." ~ **Benjamin Franklin.**

I am a trained commercial pilot. I was taught that air travel is the safest means of transportation. Yet I was trained in all types of emergencies that can lead to plane crash. The fact that planes do crash occasionally did not negate the fact that air travel is the safest. The fact that air travel is the safest does not negate the fact that pilots are trained in all types of emergencies. Not training pilots for emergencies because air travel is the safest will not be considered smart. However, it is training pilots for all kind of emergencies that makes air travel the safest. After all, the best safety device in an aircraft is a well trained pilot. Apply the same concept to your money management and you are more likely than not to enjoy the simple pleasures that life has to offer in your old age.

In my journey through life, I made shipload of mistakes. But I may not have made some of those mistakes had I have proper guidance. My constant warning that we must strive to do the right things the right way, even if not in all things, but in most things, and, even if not at all times, but most of the time, is a legitimate child of my early life's mistakes. Early in life, I was calm but reckless with money. But now I am calm and careful. That is why I make mistakes less and less and less. It is better late than never. A Dutch proverb says, we get old too quick and get smart too late. This proverb applies to me. I had already made all the mistakes I could make before becoming "awakened". Do not make the same mistake if age is still on your side. Get smart. Get awakened. Get proper guidance, the inner one is my preference. However, it requires self-discipline and self-control.

This is indeed a trying time for a lot of people, a time of adversity for some. Recession was here. They said it has gone. Has it? Inflation, weakened currency, and incessant killings continue to dance in our midst. In the midst of this adversity, there are opportunities. This time of adversity can truly lead to the determination to do away with the wrong decisions, false beliefs, and negative mentality that led one into this adversity, keeping one glued to poverty. Are you drinking, partying away the money for a piece of land? If emergency comes, can you simply dip hands into your pocket to take care of it? Is your social capital an asset or liability? Subordinating what you want now for what you want later is one of the habits of highly effective people. Saving money for rainy days is foundational to future living, loving and laughing. So is "cutting your coat according to your fabrics." Of course you have freedom of choice. But those choices have natural, immutable, sometimes unintended, consequences. Even though you do not have the direct freedom to choose the consequences of your free choices, you have the indirect freedom to choose consequences when you are exercising your freedom of choice. Incompetence is a choice. So also is corruption. "Corruption is dishonest actions that destroys people's trust in the person or group, like the news of corruption in how your bank is run, that makes you close your account and invest your money somewhere else. The noun corruption comes from Latin — com, or "with, together," and rumpere, meaning "to break." Corruption breaks your trustworthiness, your good reputation with others. When you corrupt something that is pure or honest, you take away those qualities... Corruption is "lack of integrity or honesty (especially susceptibility to bribery); use of a position of trust for dishonest gain. It is the "inducement (as of a public official) by improper means (as bribery) to violate duty (as by committing a felony). And it is the "decay of matter (as by rot or oxidation)" Using archaic belief system is a choice. Wasteful spending on ceaseless celebrations is a choice. Saving for rainy days, cutting coat according to fabrics are choices. And they all have natural, immutable, sometimes unintended consequences. So also is "doing the right things at the right times...." Integrity is no simple matter. It is very easy for people to lie when trying to make money. Once you start lying or condone lying, you are headed for serious trouble. This is the right time to bid poverty goodbye forever. This is the right time to develop The Millionaire Mindset.

To be successful tomorrow requires learning and development today. It requires laying the block of success, today, one block at a time, for tomorrow's success. To be successful tomorrow, focus on developing your human capitals instead of just settling for a life of perpetual poverty. Waiting for the government, in a lot of cases, is not realistic hope. To reiterate, "Human capital is the stock of knowledge, habits, social and personality attributes, including creativity, embodied in the ability to perform labor so as to produce economic value." You must sacrifice to get pertinent knowledge and skills. You must shrink their appetites and distend your scruples. You must associate with valuable friends and cultivate a pleasing personality. Finally, you must be creative and innovative. By focusing on developing and increasing your human capitals, all the other capitals, of which financial is one, will be yours on the long run." The only reason the season of mango will yield mango fruits is if a mango tree was already standing ahead of the season..." ~ **Olajide Abiola**. In order to collect money for house rent, one must have, at a time in the past, buy a piece of land and build a house on it, or buy a completed house, if one did not inherit one from parents.

Let us live within our means. Let us be proactive and innovative, practical and prudent, with our finances. And let us remember those that are genuinely poor because of the cards that life has dealt to them. Those stuffs that we have not used in the last six months let us give them out to those who truly need them. Simply, let us be the answer to someone else prayer.

Being sound and healthy in mind and body contributes to your success and happiness. If you are healthy, you'll be able to think more clearly, so you can make better decisions and exercise better judgment when doing your work. Make it a point to exercise regularly. Eat your meals properly and maintain a balanced diet. Sound health begins with a sound health consciousness, just as financial success begins with a prosperity consciousness.

Developing and establishing positive habits leads to peace of mind, health and financial security. You are where you are because of your established habits and thoughts and deeds. Think of salary and savings as tools to escape poverty. However, they are short-term solutions to creating wealth. Even though they are very fundamental, the majority of the people cannot create wealth with salary and savings alone. Salary and savings will manage poverty, but may not cure it. Do not just manage poverty; cure it by developing the millionaire mindset.

Those who live above their means cannot get rich by legitimate means. They will always beg, borrow, or steal. Stealing is not the best way to make money because it exposes the human life to irreparable danger. Begging is not because it erodes inner confidence. Selling is. Selling is the "last step in the chain of commerce where a buyer exchanges cash for a seller's good or service, or the activity of trying to bring this about." ~ **BusinessDictionary.com.**

There are places or people that make us want to spend a little too much. We ought to limit our contact with those places and people so we can learn to spend only what we have planned to spend. Eating out when you have food at home is one way to spend money that could be saved. Having more children than your income can support is an irresponsible act. It is an invitation to future crisis. Learn how to shrink your social obligations to a manageable proportion that your pocket can accommodate. Limit social activities that eat into your savings without bringing added income. We all make money so that we can spend money. But make sure you spend a nice chunk of your money on economic activities that will yield future returns. We get good at habits, whether good habits or bad habits, through repetition.

I have ceaselessly written about how we should cut our coat according to our fabrics. But before we can even attempt to cut the coat according to the fabrics, it is very vital to have acquired the fabrics first. Every human being is capable of making money to sustain himself or herself. But it requires systematic knowledge and training. Every society has its own unique needs and wants. Find what those needs and wants, then, develop yourself, your competence, to the level where you can, not only meet those needs and wants, but also exceed them. Simply put, become useful to yourself and your society.

I was an expert at throwing money away. So I can sure teach you how not to throw your money away. Before I make any decision these days, I first of all do the ethical and financial analysis. Is the decision ethical? If someone else does that same thing I am about to do to me or for me, will I like it? Can my pocket sustain the decision and not pass the financial responsibility to others? If the answer is yes on both counts, I go ahead and decide, and of course execute the decision. Cultural and religious factors no longer play major roles in my financial decision making.

Follow these simple steps and you cannot go wrong: discover your talents. Acquire the necessary knowledge to develop your talents. Develop the pertinent skills to utilize your talents and knowledge. Know what you want out of life. And focus on it. Know how to use your talents, knowledge and skills to get what you want out of life. Gain the mastery of success and happiness. Put your talents, knowledge, and skills to better yourself, your family, your country. And, always remember that most decisions have financial implications. Analyze the financial implications thoroughly before making any decision. Plans work more effectively when the money issues associated with the plans have been resolved. Make effective decisions. Seal that leak in your pocket. Save more. Invest more. Spend less. Those who call you selfish, stingy now will come and beg you for money later.

The more fulfilling activities you engage in, the more money you are going to spend, and the less disposable income you are going to have. Well, that may not be a bad thing if the fulfilling activities are largely economic activities that will yield future returns. But if they are largely social activities without significant financial returns, that, folks, may not be too good on the long run. Is this not the reason why a lot of people beg for money instead of cutting their coat according to their fabrics or out rightly doing without? Some of us have learned how to shrink our social obligations to a manageable proportion that our pocket can accommodate. But the majority has not. They want to keep on doing as it has always been done, even if they have to transfer the financial burden to other people, because they cannot afford it.

In order to have extra cash at hand, one must either increase income by any means possible, or reduce expenses by any means necessary. The easiest of the two, for me, in Nigeria, is to reduce my expenses by shrinking my appetites, by reducing my financial burdens. This is why I begged to be exempted from all the cultural/religious never ending celebrations. I may have been a chicken at one point, but now I am a bird. I can fly, figuratively.

This is what life experience has taught me. One of the surest ways to indulge in worrying and stressing is to accept more financial liabilities than our income can conveniently accommodate. Not only will this stress us and make us worry, it will also take a toll on our vital relationships. A worry-free, stress-free lifestyle is an essential ingredient in the pot of happiness. Be a good cook. Make that pot of happiness delicious. Make it lasting for eternal consumption.

9 789785 634303